TAUNTON CASEBOOK

Lynda Hotchkiss

For the PRIORSWOOD COMMUNITY CENTRE
Eastwick Road, Taunton

Published in 2022 by FeedARead.com Publishing

INDEX

DEDICATED TO ALL WHO MANAGE, RUN AND VOLUNTEER
AT THE PRIORSWOOD COMMUNITY CENTRE
AND
TO ALL WHO ATTEND MEETINGS AND CLASSES THERE, OR
SIMPLY DROP-IN FOR A CUPPA AND A CHAT

1.   THE SEALEY SISTERS

Interest in this event was raised by an article in the *Taunton Courier &
Western Advertiser* (8 April 1944 edition) in an item looking back at
local events of the past. Under the "100 years ago" banner, the
following was noted:

"Faith and Mary Ann Sealey were indicted at the Lent Assizes at Taunton for
the murder of their father, William, at Kingston on 20 April 1843 by
administering arsenic to him, causing his death of 23 April.
At 6a.m., the great yard was crammed with persons, and hundreds went
away, giving up all hopes of obtaining admission to the court but still the yard
was full through the whole of the day, and the court was full as soon as the
doors opened. A subscription had been raised for their defence. The Jury in a
few minutes found them Not Guilty.
Mary Ann Sealey was then indicted for the wilful murder of Betty Sealey, also
at Kingston, on 8 December 1843 by squeezing and pressing her hand upon
her throat, thereby strangling her. After about one hour's deliberation, the jury
found her Not Guilty.
The trial occupied the attention of the court from 9a.m. to 8p.m. On bringing
the prisoner out of court, the multitude set up a frightful cry of execration,
which pursued the van nearly all the way to the gaol."

Getting away with patricide? And who was the other victim, Betty
Sealey? What did "execration" actually mean? As usual, lots of
questions in need of answers.
The last was possibly the easiest. The 19th century reporters often used
words that have either no need of in today's society or refers to
something we no longer have or use. They possibly thought adding
these descriptions would show their skill at reporting accurately for
their readers, and making sure those who had only a smattering of
education would be in awe of their finished articles. According to the
Merriam-Webster dictionary, "execration" is a noun meaning the act
of cursing or denouncing, and/or an object of curse or something to be
detested. Clearly, the reporter in 1844 thought the crowd detested the
Sealey sisters for getting away with murder.
The death of William Sealey came next in priority as it happened
before Betty's death. With the help of an article in the *Leamington
Courier* (3 Feb 1844 edtn) with the headline "Charge of Parricide at

Taunton" it was possible to gain information about William and his death from the coroner's inquest report. William's body was exhumed from the grave in Kingston churchyard and an inquest held after the circumstances surrounding the death of Betsy Sealey came to light, in the house adjoining that occupied by the two Sealey sisters.

The corpse of William Sealey was scrutinised as to the exact cause of his death whilst it reposed temporarily in the church tower of Kingston parish church. Clearly the authorities were not going to pay for a cadaver to be taken somewhere more suited for a post mortem, and it meant less hassle for all concerned when disposing of the same once everything was completed.

William Sealey was described as between 40 and 50 years of age and his general health was not good but he was still able to work as a labourer in husbandry. He was regarded as a man of good character who was an attendee at the Independent chapel in Kingston St Mary. The first witness at the inquest was a medical man named Herapath told the inquest that he found two ulcers of long-standing on William's legs. This is likely to have been William Herapath (1796-1868) who was born in Bristol and had given medical evidence in other trials, including the infamous William Palmer of Rugeley (Staffs) in 1856. Herapath was also one of the founders of the Chemical Society of London, and of the Bristol Medical School, where he served as professor of chemistry and toxicology from its opening in 1828.

The second witness was William's son, Thomas, who worked at Pickney near the family's home. He made it clear to the coroner that one James Bond – no, not the 007 kind, merely a farm labourer – would visit the house occasionally, but whose visits increased in frequency after William's death, to the point of spending the whole night there in the same bed as Thomas' sister, Mary.

The re-burial of William was completed without further ceremony but Faith and Mary Sealey, daughters of the deceased, were suspected of hastening his death, though nothing was attributed to them at the time of their father's demise. A short time later, another member of the Sealey family was found dead, and this time there certainly were suspicious circumstances.

The later inquest stated that the second victim, Betty Sealey, was an aunt to the two sisters, and Mary was committed to gaol for Betty's death but was suspected of taking some part in her father's death, for which her sister was also committed. Mary was dressed in half-mourning at this inquest and described as being very much agitated by the proceedings, whereas her sister was less so.

Faith Sealey, the co-accused with her sister, Mary, apparently confessed to the crime of patricide, saying that her sister had asked her before their father's demise if she had made up her mind about going to Taunton. This is likely to have been a reference to working as a servant, which Faith certainly did as soon as her father died. That might look a little suspicious to modern minds but Victorian households could take their pick of young females needing to be employed in domestic service, and if one candidate failed to appear to take up a position, it was easy to find a replacement. Clearly Faith needed the work, and dared not miss her chances.

Faith recounted that Mary wished her to buy something from Taunton but would not reveal what it was until Faith was leaving home for the town. After making the decision to depart Kingston on the Monday morning, Mary then asked Faith to purchase a pennyworth of arsenic, stating it could be acquired from a Mr Joyce's establishment when Faith asked where such a substance could be obtained. Mary knew this was a feasible transaction as she had purchased it there several times before.

We have to remember that arsenic was seen as an everyday object, like we use bleach today, and it proved to be most effective against rats and other vermin in the 19th century.

Mary urged her sister to have someone go with her to Mr Joyce's establishment but Faith said she didn't know anybody except a Mr Green's servant, later identified as Ann Richards who lived at Bishops Lydyard. There was some discussion between the two sisters over who should accompany Faith on her mission, and how the transaction should take place, with Faith unsure of being allowed to buy arsenic, while Mary insisted she should say it was to deal with rats. Faith claimed that she commented she had not heard any rats in the house, to which Mary retorted she wouldn't hear anything if a wagon and horses drove through the bedroom. Perhaps Faith was a heavy sleeper, or …

Faith duly went to Taunton where she visited the Half Moon public house at 36 North Street* where she met Ann Richards and asked her to accompany her to buy the arsenic. Ann refused, saying she was too

*36 North Street lies next to Whirligig Place and is occupied (2020) by a mobile phone shop

busy, but one of her fellow-servants went with Faith instead. The chemist, Mr Bleadon, refused to sell to Faith without she produced a written note stating what it was to be used for. Naïvely, Faith said she didn't know its purpose and it wasn't for her. Categorically refusing the transaction, Faith then went to Mr Joyce's establishment where a young boy was behind the counter. Despite him asking all the right questions, and Faith repeating what she had said previously, she managed to purchase the arsenic in three single wraps before returning to the Half Moon Inn, where she remained for ten minutes or so before returning home to give the substance to Mary. Faith's confession stated that her sister, Mary, put the arsenic packets into her pocket.

William Sealey was fond of salt fish – usually cod that has been dried and salted, and needs soaking before being cooked. On the Thursday before his death, it was given to him for his meal along with milt (the reproductive gland of a male fish). Faith stated that she saw Mary sprinkle the poison onto the milt but said nothing to their father as he ate it. William commented that the fish did not taste as good as other times he had eaten it, and he then imbibed a pipe of tobacco before going out to work again. He was employed as a farm labourer but came home for dinner at lunchtime. He returned home that particular evening, when Faith was in their garden, and he sat at the table asking Mary for a cup of tea. A little later, before going to bed, he asked Mary if she had any arrowroot or something similar, the sort of thing that might settle an upset stomach. Faith again declared that Mary mixed up a little arrowroot for him and he seemed to improve, but half an hour after they retired to bed, William was definitely worse. The two girls left him all that night, and next morning, he again asked Mary to make him a cup of tea – typical of a working man's early morning cuppa. He then requested Mary go to Mr Mortimer (presumably the local doctor) to ask him to call. Mortimer duly obliged and ordered some type of remedy to make William feel well again, requesting Mary come to his home to collect it.
Despite the doctor's medicine, William continued to get suffer and deteriorate, especially after taking the prescribed remedy, which was administered to him by his said daughter.
The next morning, Mary again went to Mr Mortimer and was given several more powders for her father along with a bottle of something. She was given instructions as to how to mix the powders with the liquid and it was to be drunk while still hot. The newspapers didn't

bother explaining what this concoction might have been … probably because everyone would have been familiar with the sort of remedy being given, a bit like today, we all understand aspirin or paracetamol helps get rid of a headache, among other ailments.

Back in the family home, Mary did as instructed by Mr Mortimer, and then took three of the medicinal powders upstairs. She was gone for several minutes, and her father enquired why she did not return to sit sewing alongside Faith. He asked Faith to go and see what Mary was about, and on entering the room, Faith noticed her sister was near the dresser, on which reposed three opened packets of powder and the three packets of arsenic Faith had obtained previously at Mary's behest. Faith recounted that their father was angry at Mary's absence but Mary just dismissed her, telling her to go back downstairs. Without being able to hear the tone in Mary's voice, this not only sounds somewhat dismissive, but it also suggests that Mary was up to no go, and wanted to keep her actions as secretive as possible.

Mary joined Faith downstairs a little later, and she was apparently in possession of three packets of powders … but which three? The doctor's remedy, the poison, or a mixture of both?

Faith noticed that those three particular packets were stowed separately from the doctor's medicine, as if to ensure Mary knew which ones to give to their father. When she made up the required remedy, Faith noticed that the powders "did not boil up", possibly meaning the reaction of the medicine was different to before. William took this medicine - and felt even worse than ever.

Taking another concoction a little later, one that was three times the dose given before, it made him so sick that he refused any further medication. His condition worsened thereafter until he eventually died, though he did managed to drink three cups of tea in that time.

Faith Sealey's confession was unsigned. She was remanded, and her sister brought into court to be told that whatever her sibling had told the inquiry, it did not affect her. Mary was described as appearing weak and affected by the situation, and she had nothing to say on the matter beyond her sister, Faith, had got it wrong.

Summing up the evidence, the coroner duly waited for the jury to arrive at their verdict. They took all night, and returned to the court at about three in the morning. They had decided that William Sealey had been wilfully murdered by his two daughters, and both females would

9

now face further legal proceedings that would ultimately result in sentence being passed.

In April of 1844, the whole of Taunton was agog when the Sealey sisters were brought to answer to the law of the land. The salacious idea that two girls could consort together to do away with their father saw hundreds of people trying to get inside the courtroom to hear things first-hand. Those unable to be in the courtroom waited at the entrance, hoping to hear juicy snippets of what was happening.
The hall was so quiet that the tip-tapping of the prisoners' boots could be heard before either of them came into view. Described as two plain country-looking young women, they entered a joint plea of Not Guilty. Their defence by Mr Kingslake and Mr Edwards initially requested that they be tried separately. The prosecution – Mr Carey and Mr Mereweather - made no objection to this, and Mary was removed from the dock. The case against Faith was heard first.

The court was shown William Sealey's stomach, now empty of food but covered in a yellow-coloured pasty-like matter. This matter had been subjected to the best tests of the time and it was deduced to be yellow sulphuret of arsenic, also known as orpiment. It was stated that this was an indication that the victim had been subjected to large quantities of arsenic shortly before his death. The arsenic ingested would turn into orpiment immediately after death, and this poison caused the inflammation that was regarded to be the cause of death. Mary was not tried for her father's murder, and was therefore acquitted of that charge, because Mr Carey as the prosecutor felt the particular matter had already been fully investigated.

According to a lengthy piece in the *Sherborne Mercury* (13 Apr 1844 edtn), and headlined "The Taunton Murders" a lot more information was recorded. It stated that twenty year old Faith Sealey was charged with administering white arsenic to her father at Pinckney in the parish of Kingston, rendering him sick and distempered, and ultimately he died on 23rd of April. A second count charged her with aiding and abetting the same offence. This somehow seems to be at odds with her account of events leading up to her father's death, as well as somehow contradicting each other. If she was the one who allegedly administered the poison to William Sealey, how can she also "aid and abet" in the same matter? If Faith only aided and abetted in her

10

father's poisoning, there should be another perpetrator who actually conceived the plan … shouldn't there?

There followed evidence from 27 witnesses, including several of Faith's family – siblings Thomas (age 12), John (14), William (16), Sarah (10) and James, the latter having been summoned to the family property when their father was stricken. Other witnesses included William Herapath of Bristol, a couple of local doctors, the police, and folk who attested to how Faith acquired the arsenic, what they saw or knew about the family along with their personal impressions of the relationship between the sisters and their father. One witness, a Charlotte Tucker, a resident in Kingston, regaled the court with an incident in which the two Sealey sisters were at a local hostelry on the "Monday after Lady Day" when their father came in and told them to return home. Shaking his stick at them, he left them on the premises after they refused to do as he bid, despite his obvious anger at their presence there. Remember James Bond? The man who visited occasionally and - after William Sealey's death - managed to stay many nights in Mary's bed; he confirmed Charlotte's account of the same incident and admitted he had been keeping company with Mary ever since. What a lovely term for being the boyfriend of Mary!

Chemist John Beadon related how Faith came to his shop to buy arsenic - which he sold at a penny for half an ounce – and how he would never sell such an item to anyone he did not know. He was followed by John Joyce, chemist and druggist, who admitted that at the time Faith visited his premises, he definitely had a large quantity of arsenic in stock, and that any he sold would always be marked "Poison". His shopboy, Aaron Bamfield (17 at the time of the trial) gave his short evidence, claiming he could not remember the incident in which he allegedly sold the poison to Faith Sealey. Convenient memory lapse, or what?

The first to give more detailed evidence was one William Westcombe, a carpenter at Kingston, who had known William Sealey and attended his funeral. He told the court that William's grave was opened on January 18th 1844 and the coffin removed into the church's belfry. As the gravedigger for the parish, he said the coffin looked the same as when it had gone into the grave cut Westcombe had dug to receive it. It was in the belfry that various parts of the body were taken away, including the whole of the stomach and the intestines. They were placed in an earthenware pot and sealed before being taken for what we would call today "forensic testing".

The matter of what Faith had said once she was interrogated initially was also brought out by questioning the relevant individuals. However, objections were made to such evidence from a policeman, and by a solicitor concerning her confession.

However, the Governor of the gaol was heard by the court. Faith's statement of events was read out and finally, the judge summed everything up for the jury.

The jury took only twenty minutes to find Faith Sealey Not Guilty of her father's murder. That was probably a fair summary since nothing given in her trial could prove the Faith had administered any noxious substance to anyone. The evidence only confirmed that she had purchased some arsenic whilst in Taunton, and then only because her sister requested it.

Next day, it was Mary's turn in court. She is often shown as Mary Ann Sealey rather than the Mary she was baptised. She had been charged with her father's murder but discharged of that offence because the prosecutor felt all the evidence had been heard during Faith's case. There was a second charge of the murder of Betty Sealey on 8 December 1843 by strangulation. Who was this Betty Sealey? This was the first occasion that name had appeared as it had not been mentioned in any context with Faith's trial.

This seems to be an appropriate point to look at the Sealey family involved in all of this.

Faith and Mary were the daughters of the unfortunate William Sealey and a number of their siblings gave evidence in court. William had married a Mary Phillips in 1818, by whom he had fathered ten children before his wife's untimely death in 1842 at 45 years of age. William's burial records his age as also 45 years, placing his birth to about 1794. His baptism in the Kingston St Mary parish registers records the surname as "Cealy", and his parents as Thomas and Betty. Surnames often go through a variety of spellings, dependent on the pronunciation given and the clerk's education … or lack of it. Thomas and Betty were married in the same parish in 1786, and her maiden name was Yea – a surname associated with Pyrland Hall, which is very close to the parish of Kingston. Whether Betty has any connection to the family at the Hall remains speculative.

Thomas and Betty had two other children – a daughter they called Betty in 1787 and son James in 1790. The said James married in 1813 to a Betty Kibby, by whom he had a number of children (including George, whose son William Sealey (1846-1918) was innkeeper at The Crown, 62 High Street, Taunton at the close of the 19th century).

Not only is there a Betty Sealey as grandmother to the two sisters charged with the murder of a Betty Sealey, Mary and Faith also have two aunts bearing that name – one apparently remaining as a spinster and who was their father's sister; the other the wife of their father's brother. A fourth contender called Betty Sealey was baptised in 1785 at Kingston, daughter of James & Faith Sealey, brother and sister-in-law to Thomas & Betty (Yea) and uncle and aunt to the murdered William. One of these poor unfortunates must be the murdered female mentioned in the charges against Mary.

The Kingston registers record the burial of a Betty Sealey on 17th of December 1843, only eight months after William's demise, and her age is given as 80. This places her birth to around 1763, and thereby eliminates William's sister (born about 1787), William's cousin (born about 1785) and probably his sister-in-law, Betty (nee Kibby), since she married a man born in 1790. That leaves only the oldest of the four Betty's – the sisters' grandmother. Is it possible to have a crime known as grandmatricide?

In December 1843, seventy-nine year old Betty Sealey was found dead in an upstairs closet. She was thought to have been strangled. There had been several thefts of food from her larder, and a removable floorboard was found in an upstairs room that allowed access into Betty's cupbard from another part of the building. The upstairs room was occupied by Betty's great-nieces - or grand-daughters - Mary Sealey (22) and her sister, Faith (18). The three women resided in an old farm-house at Pickney in the parish of Kingston St Mary which had been divided into two separate dwellings. Betty, described as their aunt bot probab;y their grandmother, did not get on very well with the young Sealey girls, and neither of them showed any remorse once Betty was known to be dead. It was the inquest into Betty's death that led to the exhumation of William Sealey's body, father of the same two females that shared Betty's building. Hope you are following all this …

So, Mary Sealey was indicted for the wilful murder of her father, and her grandmother, except the grandmother was described as her aunt, but the prosecution declined to offer any evidence in the first case, and she was acquitted of that crime. It is possible that because her sister had confessed to taking part in their father's death and had duly been acquitted that it was going to be an uphill battle to prove it was all Mary's doing. Instead, the court listened to the second charge of murder by strangulation. This time it took 29 witnesses to reveal all the facts relevant to the case, and again, members of Mary's family found themselves in the witness-box.

The first witness, who was not a relative, had been tasked with creating a model of the property in which the family lived. They occupied an old former farmhouse in Kingston. It had been divided to provide two dwellings – one for the two sisters and their siblings, and the other for grandmother Betty. Due to its' age, the floorboards were in a parlous state and, after inspecting the scene of the crime, it was found that a portion of the boards were removable, enabling those in a particular bedroom to see down into the room below. In fact, they could view the outer door of the lower room's pantry, and even reach inside to help themselves to supplies.

Betty's grandson, John Sealey, gave his evidence, stating that he went with his father (the deceased William who had succumbed to poison had a son who was named John) and a man named George Yeo (who might be related to the murdered woman, because her name could easily be Yeo or Yea) to Pinckney between seven and eight o'clock at night on 9th of December, retrieving the key to Betty's property from a neighbour. The witness's father, John Sealey Senior (and brother to the deceased William), unlocked the door and called out to his mother. Receiving no response, the trio went upstairs where they found her sitting on a chair with her head leaning towards her right shoulder and wearing her bonnet and cloak. Young John saw marks on the woman's throat, and her tongue hanging out of her mouth. Just as they were moving the body, Mary arrived and asked "Is the old creature killed?". Despite many changes in the language we use today compared to that in 1844, this seems a very strange thing to say.

A minute or so later, Mary went into her own quarters. John Senior's evidence stated that there was no sign of a struggle, and that Mary told him the following morning that she had last seen old Betty during the morning of her death "when she was going for her pay". Women often worked well into their seventies or eighties but some were entitled to

14

parish relief … a sort of dole money cum old age pension that was paid to them by the parish, providing they had lived in the parish long enough to qualify for the same. Saying Betty was going for her pay was probably a reference to Betty receiving some form of support, either from her parish or, more porbably, from the Union.

Unions were groups of parishes who collaborated in building the large imposing workhouses that appear in Victorian literature, such as Charles Dickens' "Oliver Twist". Whilst the poor, sick, elderly and disabled were encouraged to enter these institutions, selected individuals were allowed to remain in their homes and would go regularly to receive some form of relief in cash, bread or coal.

John Senior's wife, Betty Sealey, then gave her account. She had certainly seen old Betty after her demise, but the last time she saw her alive was the day before her death. Betty the wife had handed a neighbour old Betty's half pint gin bottle, presumably refilled or for topping it up. Clearly, old Betty enjoyed a regular tipple. Betty the wife agreed that Mary had made that strange comment, but her version of Mary's words was "Is the poor dear soul murdered?" She refused to swear that Mary had used the word "killed" rather than "murdered" but either way, it was a very strange thing for a grand-daughter to ask.

George Yea added more mystery to the whole matter by mentioning that when Mary came into the house, she was wearing a black bonnet and a dark shawl, garments she was not wearing when she came back downstairs and that she had gone up the stairs without using a light. Perhaps he wondered why she was moving about in the dark when the floors were so hazardous - yet, if Mary was familiar with the property where her grandmother resided, she would not need to light her way, and wasn't it fairly common to put your outer garments into your bedroom in a home with multiple occupants?

The house where the Sealeys resided was not owned by them, but instead belonged to a Robert Farthing, whose sister-in-law, Elizabeth, held the spare key.

Charlotte Hay stepped into the witness box to give her account of Betty and her pay from Kingston Union – the poor relief referred to earlier. Apparently, Charlotte had gone and collected Betty's allowance on her behalf. This seems to be at odds with Mary's intimation that she watched old Betty set off to claim this benefit. Charlotte went to give it to Betty about 8pm, finding the door locked and no-one would answer. She said that she sent George Yeo to seek entry that evening, and was with him when he gained access into Betty's home. Strange that the two Sealey men failed to mention Charlotte's presence in their evidence … unless the reporter just didn't bother to write her name down in his notebook. Charlotte was also there when the medical man arrived to examine the body, and she took Betty's "pocket" – or purse, as we would refer to it today – and found the door-key inside it but the drawstrings were broken rather than untied. The gin bottle she had fetched the night before for old Betty was not found in the house, despite Charlotte searching everywhere. The relevance of this bottle of gin seems lost in the overall severity of the alleged murder, but somehow, it keeps cropping up as a crucial piece of evidence. Perhaps its relevance was its absence at the scene of the crime, and that it could only have been removed by the person or persons that caused old Betty's death.

The medical man who examined old Betty's corpse, Francis Welch, surgeon, recounted seeing a mark on the female's left cheek rather than on her jawbone, and on the left side of her windpipe were marks that gave the impression of fingers pressing down. There was also a mark on the right side of the throat, again thought to have been caused by pressure, possibly from a thumb. Either her assailant applied pressure from behind, with the right arm placed over the victim's right shoulder to cause such bruising, if indeed these marks are relevant to Betty's cause of death, or alternatively, if the woman was held by the throat from the front, again the attacker had to be right-handed.
The mark on the right side of the windpipe had drawn some blood and Welch had seen blood on the left doorpost about two feet from the ground. There were further marks on the right forearm, a small triangular wound on the right elbow that also showed blood, and four similar marks on the inside of Betty's right wrist with two slight marks on her side. He categorically said that such marks – probably deep bruises – could not occur after death, but it was possible that, if the old lady had a fit, she might feel she was being suffocated and raise her hands to her throat to try to breathe more easily. The blood he had seen on the doorpost was likely to have occurred when the men carried her body out of the room where she was found. How much pressure would it require for an old woman to put her right hand onto her throat in the hope of breathing more easily? Surely, there would come a point where the pain of her own hand would have outweighed the desire to clutch at her throat in a vain attempt to ease what the surgeon was

16

suggesting as simply some sort of fit. The slight signs of blood described do not seem sufficient to smear on doorposts, but no description of the amount of blood is reported. Oh, for today's CSI to have existed in 1844, with cameras to capture blood spatter, the position of the body, etc.

Another witness, Gabriel Porter, overheard a conversation between the victim and her landlord, in which old Betty said she had been robbed. Betty told Porter to "move on", to which Gabriel presumed that she had some secret about him that she intended to tell to the landlord, Farthing. Porter's evidence is somewhat out of place. He remarks Betty had said she had been robbed (of some wood, as it turned out) and adds it was unlikely she would say such a thing if it had not actually happened. He then refers to "false keys" being in somebody's possession so that they could access Betty's premises whenever they wanted. He also told the court that Mary Sealey had told him that her grandmother was "a durned bad old woman". Was he there to add weight to the case against Mary, or does his information imply an unknown third party was targeting Betty, and had unlimited access to the old lady's home because they had some form of duplicate key?

Other witnesses recounted their little bits of information and hearsay about seeing Betty, what Mary said to them, and reference was made to a hawker paying Mary a visit. The hawker told the court that he had intend called on Mary but that she hadn't purchased any of his wares, so he went off towards Bishops Lydeard about two and a half miles away, and took an hour to walk it.
Remember James Bond who was extremely … shall we say "friendly" … with the accused Mary Sealey? Well, his mother, Mary Bond, gave evidence that the said Mary Sealey had come to do some washing for her (Bond) because Bond was suffering a bad leg. Her statements really do nothing more than confirm James and Mary had got something going between them, and that he was often away from his home overnight.
Mary's younger brother, another John Sealey, was called to give evidence but nothing he told the court pointed the finger at or away from his sister, and again that missing gin bottle was mentioned.

John Burford, a policeman at Taunton, reiterated the information about the removable floorboard that gave access to the room and larder below, adding that he spotted a small bit of white cotton hanging from it after it had been moved for examination. There was also something red on the top of the door below that he could not identify beyond it was possibly cotton and very small. Nobody took the time to ask or describe the clothes Mary Sealey was wearing the night her dead grandmother was found beyond a black bonnet and dark shawl. For that matter, nobody who was in the house for the three days leading to old Betty's killing, nor those finding the deceased, had their clothes brought into question for elimination. Mary had lost her father a few months earlier, even if she was responsible for his death, and would be wearing black as a sign of mourning, though black was quite a common colour for bonnets and shawls. Well … black goes with just about anything, doesn't it?

When the acting Superintendent of Police, one William Richard Hitchcock, a surgeon-dentist in Taunton by trade, was called to give his evidence, the whole thing went back to that gin bottle. He had cautioned, interrogated, and subsequently arrested Mary Sealey and then unlocked two boxes in a bedroom where he found the missing gin bottle. This bottle was identified by Charlotte Hay as the one she had supplied to old Betty but the relevance of this information is still lost in the overall scheme of things, especially as the occupant of the bedroom in which the bottle was found is never named in the newspaper reports. Likewise, what was the relevance of the Inspector of Police, a William Samuels, finding three fourpenny pieces and a shilling under the bedpost in Mary's bedroom when he re-examined the room on December 19th ? The relieving officer for Kingston Union said that he had paid out old Betty's money in fourpenny pieces, which implies that Mary had stolen the money from her grandmother's pocket after strangling her and cutting Betty's purse-strings to take it. Why did Samuels feel the need to return to the scene of the crime after four days, and only then notice these hidden coins? Could someone else be responsible for secreteing them under the bedpost? Chances are, once the police left and the corpse removed, that room was once again used by the family. The concept of selaing off the crime scene until all evidence therein had been gathered is very much a part of modern criminal procedure.

This is turning into a "he said, she said" battle of evidence with a gin bottle and coins having more emphasis placed upon them than the bruises and blood on the corpse.

The prosecution then called witnesses that put the cap on the whole thing. First it was Rebecca Dimock, who was in Wilton Gaol for misconduct when Mary Sealey was brought in on remand. Dimock is supposed to have mentioned to Mary that a girl had just arrived there on a charge of murder, and Mary had snapped back "Hold your tongue!". While in sick bay, Dimock was again in Mary's company and told the court that Mary had whined that she had destroyed her own aunt … except it wasn't Mary's aunt but her grandmother who had died. Dimock then asked Mary why she had done it, and Mary supposedly replied that when people get to that age, they ought to die, and repeated it again later. Should Dimock be believed that Mary had confessed to killing her grandmother, especially after being cross-examined and revealing that she, Rebecca Dimock, had been in Wilton Gaol five times in the previous two years?

Dimock was followed by Rebecca Woodland, who was in the same gaol with her daughter when Mary was brought in. There was chit-chat between them about a letter from her (Mary's) uncle and that flipping bottle again. Woodland was also cross-examined in court and it was revealed that she was then in gaol on the same charge as her daughter, receiving money that Woodland's sons had stolen while in Taunton market. Interestingly, Woodland had already had three of her children sentenced to be transported while she had been acquitted of whatever charge they paid the penalty on.

Another prisoner, this time in Shepton Mallet Gaol, was called to retell events while she was in Wilton Gaol awaiting trial. While walking with Jane Woodland, Mary Sealey was heard by both of them saying "I thought they were dead and looked back and saw her move, and then I cut her elbow and wrist". This convict, a Julia Ann Starr, said she looked at Mary's boots and saw four nails in them. The defence must have taken umbrage at Starr's testimony, and managed to get it invalidated. Certainly, four nails in a boot is a long way from strangulation, or removable floorboards, or even from gin bottles; could be a good title for a comedy sketch though, or perhaps a piece of creative writing …

Another Woodland came into the witness box; this time a Martha Woodland who was in Wilton Gaol when the previous Julia was a prisoner there. She had also heard Mary Sealey say she went into the house while the old woman was there and that she (Mary) had left marks on her (Betty's) throat. Mary also added that the old woman was too strong for her, so Mary knocked her on the right arm and blood spurted out onto Mary's clothes. Mary is then supposed to have put four nails into the heel of one of her boots, and two in the toe of the other, so that her steps could not be tracked. Martha also stated that Mary had threatened her not to repeat a word of this to anyone. Well, that goes some way as to why the nails were mentioned before, but Mary lived next door to the victim. Her footprints would be everywhere anyway!

Blood had been found on the sleeve of Mary's dress by the Police Inspector, and his superior said the sleeve had been washed but there was still a strong stain on the inside. Neither gave the colour of the garment. Initially, newspapers made note of the fact that Mary had scratches on her hands when Betty was found dead, but this were dismissed quite quickly as not having any relevance … unless they caused the blood stains on Mary's dress. At the time, nobody put the two items - scratches and blood stained clothing - together to prove or disprove their importance or relevance in the case. You also have to question why Mary Sealey would speak so candidly, so openly to several women she didn't know in a place where everything you uttered would eventually be reported to somebody else. Perhaps these women who were keen to have their say against Mary Sealey were hoping their "helpfulness" in this matter would go well in their own trials. For someone reported to be nervous and agitated at her trial, it does not quite seem possible that she would snap "Hold your tongue" to anybody, but then again, if she was responsible for strangling an old woman, maybe there was more than one side to her … bi-polar, perhaps?

With the prosecution resting at this point, it was the turn of Mary's legal representatives to put forward on her behalf an argument to show the inaccuracy of the case against her. They chose to cover all the given evidence in some detail, but totally rubbished the three witnesses that were already incarcerated in one gaol or another, pointing out the improbability and inconsistency in their statements. The judge then took his time summing up all the evidence against Mary for the jury's benefit, and there was a twenty minute hiatus while the jury consulted further before they retired to consider their verdict. How long they deliberated was not reported, but they decided she was … Not Guilty.

The spectators waiting outside the court were horror-struck at the verdict, and soon there was a mob showing their utter dismay to the officers of the law for the verdicts of Not Guilty against either girl. An attempt was made to release the Sealey sisters from the court-house, but the mob made it impossible for them to safely leave the building as free women. Instead, they were taken back to Wilton Gaol for their own safety. There they remained for several days whilst the goodly-minded folk of Taunton raised enough funds to spirit them away from the area. Mary and Faith were later taken by railway to "one of the seaports" where they were to board a vessel that would take them to the far side of the world, to Australia. Well, two publications said Australia was their destination but the *Taunton Courier (*27 April 1844 edtn) said they were travelling to Canada.

Not being fully cognizant of how the law operated in 1844 whilst still being aware that it was nothing like it is today, it does seem very strange that Faith Sealey was charged with poisoning her father, despite her own confession suggesting she only purchased the white arsenic at her sister's insistence, and the same charge against that very sister was dropped completely. In the matter of old Betty Sealey, called an aunt when she was possibly a grandmother, Mary faces the charge of murder by strangulation and gets acquitted. Did Mary poison her father with the arsenic acquired by Faith during a visit to Taunton? Otherwise, how did the arsenic get into William's stomach unless somebody administered it with his food. With his wife barely cold in her grave, William clearly relied on his eldest two surviving daughters to fulfil the role of housewife, and to care for and raise his younger children. The youngest of the brood, Jane, was only three when her mother died, and four when she became an orphan. So what happened to the other children, the siblings of Mary and Faith?

It is always difficult when large families use the same first names among their offspring in different generations, and the Sealey family of Kingston is no different. Of those who were subjected to testifying against their sister/s in court, the oldest of them, James (baptised 1821) seems to have survived to 1871 when he was recorded on the census as a shepherd at Broomfield, a village some five miles from Taunton. Beyond that, his fate is uncertain. His younger brothers, William (baptised 1827) and John (baptised 1829) were both recorded on the 1851 census but cannot be positively identified thereafter. The same John and the youngest brother, Thomas (baptised 1832) were both put into Wilton Gaol with their sister Mary but released without charge after one week's incarceration. Thomas' fate is another mystery, and it seems highly likely that the brothers found it necessary to leave the district after Mary and Faith got away with murder. Of the three youngest siblings for the two parricides – as they were referred to in the newspaper of the day – Sarah was taken in by her aunt, Loyalty Phillips, a lodging house keeper living just off Marine Parade in Brighton and, on the 1851 census, Sarah was shown as a house servant. Perhaps she left the Taunton area once she turned twelve, the age most youngsters were expected to find employment in the 1840s. The 1861 census indicates a thirty year old Sarah Sealy claiming birth in "Somersetshire" was a parlourmaid in Hampstead, London. However, there is also a marriage for a Sarah, daughter of William Sealey (labourer), in 1859 at Huish Champflower to Francis Tout that is far more fitting. Francis died in 1864, and Sarah remarried two years later to William Stevens, who was also a widower and a labourer. The couple had three children, from whom there are living descendants in the present day. It is likely the youngest Sealey girl, Jane (baptised 1839) may have been taken in by a charitable family, given her age at the time of her sisters' departure, and could have used their surname instead of her own to dissociate herself from gossip and prejudice. Since her fate still awaits determination, it leaves only Betsy (baptised 1836). She somehow found her way into the workhouse in Taunton and died there in 1847 before being buried at Kingston.

And what of the murderous sisters, whether you believe they were guilty or innocent? Despite the good folk of Taunton donating sufficient funds for both of them to travel abroad to begin a new life, it cannot be certain if they left these shores, let alone journeyed to Australia … or should that be Canada? Nothing has been found to show either girl as a passenger on any vessel heading to either location but maybe they travelled under a new identity.

In the July of 1844, a Faith Sealey death and burial was recorded in Kingston but this is not the ill-fated girl, but her great-aunt – after whom she was probably named – the wife of James Sealey (1761-1816) and mother of several children whose fates remain at this point in time as shadowy as that of the Sealey sisters.

2. THE WOODLANDS

In the case of sisters Mary and Faith Sealey, who were charged with the murders of their grandmother and of their father respectively in 1844, the witnesses called to support the charge against them included some females - then incarcerated in Wilton Gaol - bearing the surname of Woodland. Among them was Rebecca Woodland who told the court that several of her sons had already been transported.

In the late 18th and early 19th centuries, it was a common practice to dispose of convicted prisoners who had broken the law but did not merit the death penalty by having them removed as far from England as possible. Originally, the colonies in the New World were most suitable, as labourers were required to build docks and towns as well as to work on the farms and plantations. Once the colonists rebelled against being ruled from Britain and became an independent nation called America, a new destination for these felons was sought … and found in Australia.

Rebecca fell foul of the law when one of her children, along with one William Coles, stole six notes, worth five shillings each, from a James Poole, along with another twenty shillings. Three more of her children were charged with receiving the same, knowing it to be stolen, and Rebecca with receiving only the six notes. The five members of the Woodland family and William Coles were all laborers, and appeared in the dock of the Taunton Quarter Sessions in January 1844. Whilst Coles, Rebecca and her daughter Jane were acquitted, the three boys – Joseph Woodland, age 17, James Woodland and Thomas Woodland, both aged 10 – were sentenced to be transported to Australia. Whilst this may seem a very young age to be wrenched from a family, let alone sent to a foreign land from which they were unlikely to return (providing they survived the voyage and the term of their sentences), this style of punishment among young people was a way of disposing of those who could become a bigger nuisance when they were older and were deemed to be undesirable.

Joseph Woodland was sentenced to seven years' penal servitude and left England aboard the specially commissioned vessel, *Thomas Arbuthnot*, on 6th of January 1847. For three years, he was held in either a gaol or, more likely, on the hulks, otherwise ships no longer deemed sea-worthy that were anchored off the southern shores of this country. The journey to Van Diemen's Land (now known as Tasmania) took four months, and Joseph was actually put ashore at Port Phillip where there was a penal colony. He had been baptised in Taunton in June 1829 to Thomas and Rebecca of East Reach. This implies his age was incorrect in the newspapers, and he was actually about 14 when sentenced to be transported. This would be two years above the age where he could have been employed, and it was not the first time he had been in a courtroom. In January 1843, he had been found not guilty of a charge of larceny, only to return two months later on a similar charge, for which he was sentenced to twelve days' imprisonment and to be whipped. Corporal punishment was thought to be a deterrent to those who might re-offend but Joseph was back again three months later, and again charged with a felony. Again, he was found not guilty, as was his accomplice, Thomas Coles Woodland (age 21, and his natural brother), for receiving the stolen goods. Although the newspapers described Joseph as a labourer in January 1844, the criminal records show him as a tailor or shepherd. Two completely different trades but he may have been working as a labourer looking after sheep before becoming a tailor. He was not the only Joseph Woodland to journey to the far side of the world, so his fate cannot be given here. He might be the Joseph Woodland credited with a death in 1867 at Wangaratta, Victoria, Australia.

Thomas Coles Woodland was Rebecca's son born and baptised in February 1823 in Taunton under her maiden name of Coles. Eighteen months later, Rebecca married Thomas Woodland and her son, even if her husband was not his natural father, became known by her married name. He was the first of the three transportees to leave England, sailing on board *Equestrian* on 25 January 1844 to serve a seven year sentence. The vessel arrived in Van Diemen's Land on 2 May, only a few months after another Thomas Woodland had set foot in the same place to serve the fourteen years' sentence imposed upon him at Bedford Assizes. A third Thomas Woodland had received the same term at Bristol City Sessions in 1824, arriving in New South Wales in 1825. That puts three convicts of the same name into Australia, with two of them being located in Tasmania. Determining more about them is not fully possible since little information separates them. The Taunton born Thomas could be the Thomas whose death was recorded in 1880.

24

The third deported brother was James Woodland, baptised four months after his parents were married. His father was recorded as a silk weaver of Middle Street in the 1825 baptismal entry in Taunton St James' registers. He was put on board the *Barossa* in May 1844 and the voyage was again a four month journey. In 1859, with his ten year sentence complete and freedom restored (even though he could not return to England), he married Agnes Collier (1837-1923) in Tasmania by whom he had a son, James William (1865-1924) and descendants. James died in February 1897 of an aortic aneurism, and sometimes appears in records under the same name as his son – James William Woodland.

The three transported brothers are recorded living with their parents on the 1841 census for Taunton. The family resided in East Reach and consisted of Thomas Woodland Senr who was a labourer, wife Rebecca, sons, James, Joseph and John and daughters Jane and Mary. Thomas the elder died in 1843 when he was only 43 years of age, and his demise may have contributed to the theft of James Poole's money to support the family he left behind. The 1841 census also showed another person in their household – one James Searles, a mason's journeyman.

In January 1846, Rebecca Woodland (nee Coles: she married Thomas Woodland (1800-1843) at Taunton in October 1824) married a second time at Wincanton to the same James Searle or Searles that had been living with the family in 1841. They had a daughter, Eliza, in 1849 in Devon, where James and Rebecca were living in 1851 and 1861. By 1871, they were back in Taunton at 3 Bale's Court, North Street. Rebecca died in 1878.

The daughter who was in gaol with Rebecca at the time of the Sealey sisters' trial was often mentioned as Jane, but was baptised as Martha Jane on Christmas Day 1826. In 1855, she became the wife of Samuel Searle, by whom she had children. In 1861, ironically, he was residing at 3 Fooks Court, Shuttern, Taunton and working as a guard at Taunton Gaol. He wasn't with his family in 1871 when they were living at 20 Alma Street, and 1874 they all emigrated to Australia, settling in Queensland, where Samuel died in 1875. Martha Jane married again in 1877 to a German-born widower, Hans Pieter Wieckhorst (1820-1883) and died in 1910. Among her children by her first husband was a son, James Woodland Searle, who married Emma

Woodland (1864-1898, and daughter of Martha's transported brother, Joseph) by whom there are descendants of the original subject of this section – Rebecca (Coles) Woodland, mother of three boys transported in 1844, the year she gave evidence in a murder trial at Taunton.

3. Prisoner W J HOUSE

Many a time, a crime grabs the attention of the world, or of a town such as Taunton. Nobody took a great deal of notice when a convict died, unless their death was by hanging, or occasionally, by suicide. From the *Shepton Mallet Journal* (4 Jan 1901 edtn), the following was spotted and interest roused:

" Died in Prison – An inquest was held in HM Prison on the body of William James House (50), general labourer, from the Bridgewater district, who died in prison on the previous morning from inflammation of the brain.

Henry Orpwood, principal warder and acting as chief warder in the absence of J G Barrow (Taunton Quarter Sessions) stated that the deceased was received under sentence from Taunton Assizes on 22 November for the term of two months' hard labour. He said House was not in good health at the time but did not go to the infirmary for some time after: not until ten days ago. He was certified for first class labour by the Medical Officer. He worked in his cell the whole time oakum picking on half-task. A task was one and a half pounds, and he was supposed to do three-quarters of a pound – he never completed his reduced task. Orpwood did not think the prisoner was capable of doing so, he did his best and was not pressed. He complained of pains in his head, and on several occasions, was seen by the surgeon before he went to the infirmary. He died about three o'clock on Monday morning.

The Medical Officer of the Workhouse (J T Hyatt) saw House on his arrival. On the 15th December, House complained of sleeplessness and had not said anything about pains in his head. The Medical Officer was told the prisoner had been very noisy during the night, and he had him removed to the observation cell where he continued to be noisy, stripped himself in the middle of the night and would not stay in bed. He kept House under observation for three or four days, then had him removed to the infirmary. He was then practically insane and said he saw lions in his cell. In hospital, he refused food and had to be fed by means of a stomach pump. He became insane but was unfit to be removed. The post mortem examination by the Medical Officer found the cause of death to be inflammation of the brain, which he believed was brought on by alcoholism.

House had marks on his head which he received as a blow to the head from an iron bar, and a kick from a horse. He had not been the same since, and not fully responsible for his actions.

The jury returned a verdict in accordance with medical evidence."

So why was the poor soul in prison at this time? According to the *Weston Mercury* (10 Nov 1900 edtn), William James House (50) labourer, pleaded not guilty to stealing a hay knife on 9 October at Othery. He was found guilty, and His Lordship the Judge said he (House) had been convicted twenty times since 1864 for various small matters, his heaviest sentence being six months in gaol, given when he was a boy of 15, and he would now go to Shepton Mallet gaol for two months.

Another newspaper added that the hay knife belonged to a Paul Durston and was valued at three shillings.

Now interest was piqued by those other convictions given out for "small matters" since 1864.

Thanks to the availability of criminal records on the Internet, that first conviction in 1864 was six months hard labour in Taunton Gaol for the crime of arson, and was delivered at Wells Assizes. The next discovery was seven days in Taunton Gaol from Somerset Quarter Sessions in April 1879 for obtaining £1 by false pretences from Henry Harris at Puriton just a few days earlier. House pleaded guilty to the offence, which might explain the lenient sentence. In 1886, at the Bridgewater Borough Sessions in the October, he was charged with stealing a gold ring, and got two months at hard labour. Again a mention was included that House had received twenty convictions but now listed as for trespass, assault, wilful damage, drunkenness and obscene language.

Puzzled as to why only four convictions could be located out of the twenty referred to, perhaps finding out a little more about the prisoner could be useful. With his year of death firmly established, and his age given in the inquest, it should be plain sailing to find out something about his existence.

Except, it proved harder than anticipated. Nowhere had there been any mention that William James House was born in, or lived in, the county of Somerset, although the implication was there that he came from the Bridgewater area. Unfortunately, no birth of a male with those names was registered in that location … or anywhere else in 1851. Instead, there were several contenders in Somerset alone, but their ages were anything up to ten years adrift to that quoted in 1901.

Searching further afield, if only to exclude the possible contenders, a couple of reports were found for a James House falling foul of the law.

28

Bailed from Taunton Gaol in January 1870 for making an unlawful and forcible entry on certain freehold lands and a dwelling-house at Taunton in the same month, this James House was a bailiff and the charges were ignored. However, this offence seems to be covered by the term "trespass" - as given among the list of William James House's convictions from 1864 to 1900.

Again, under the name of James House, there is reference to a 36 year old labourer being sent to serve two months' hard labour in HMP Exeter on 18 August 1886 for the theft of a gold ring worth six shillings, the property of Frank Farrow, which was stolen at Bridgewater. This certainly seems to be the man in question, with no obvious reason why he sometimes called himself William James House. The same source also adds he had been convicted to six months for arson at Wells Assizes in the summer of 1864 and another seven days in the same courts in Spring 1879 for obtaining by false pretences. The addition of this James House having received eleven convictions between 1866 and 1883 for trespass, assaults and wilful damage cements the two identities together.

Changing the search to consider James House rather than William James House, a man born about 1850 crops up on census returns for 1881 and 1891 in the employment of delivering letters whilst living in his birthplace of Stoke St Gregory. He married Sarah Ann Hunt and they produced five sons. By 1901, Sarah Ann was a widow but living in the same place as the family in the earlier census returns. Three of them can be provided with wives from obvious national sources, and two of the marriages produced issue. One has no defined fate but the youngest, Norman Stephen House, found himself on the wrong side of the law in 1914.

Norman pleaded guilty to the charge of breaking and entering a dwelling in Stoke St Gregory and stealing half a cooked fowl and half of a loaf of bread. It appeared that Norman had broken into a house where he was the lodger, despite being thrown out some time before. The householder was his brother, Rowland House, who stated that Norman was asked to leave because of "his dirty habits" whereas, Rowland's wife, Emily, claimed it was because her brother-in-law refused to work (he had previously been employed as a baker for several years but left the position and did not seek another job). The report of the court case also mentioned that Norman had become very violent and tried to escape while being placed under arrest. The doctor examining him when placed in custody gave his opinion to the court, stating that Norman was feeble-minded and on the edge of idiocy with no chance of improvement. Norman got six months for taking food from his brother's house, the house where he was staying but had been locked out on the night in question.

Five months earlier, Norman pled guilty to sleeping out, and again the court was told by the Deputy Chief Constable that he was feeble-minded and had a very slow brain. At this time, Norman had been living with his mother but she had to give up her home in the village and gone to live in London, leaving poor old Norman homeless. Brother Rowland took him in but objected to some of the habits he exhibited. On this occasion, the charge was dismissed and Norman found his way to Essex, possibly to the eldest of his brothers, and where his death was registered in 1956.

Was Norman mentally challenged, and could it have been a genetic condition inherited from his father? His mother was approaching forty when she gave birth to him, her youngest child; perhaps he suffered the condition we know as Down's Syndrome? Yet, when the First World War required men to do their patriotic duty, Norman was called to serve as Private 152639 in the Labour Corps. Enlisting in 1914 (perhaps soon after the matter of stealing food from his brother's home), Norman's discharge in 1919 records him as "insane". What nature of condition was his insanity at this time? Where did he serve? Always questions that cannot be answered unless you are a descendant of the individual involved, with family knowledge to provide a reason, but even without a solution, these small crimes are just as interesting as the large, more spectacular cases that blaze across the media of the period. It is always the little man … or woman … who is somehow driven to commit minor offences; perhaps through poverty, a need to survive or care for children, or because of a condition beyond their control. How these malefactors were treated as a means of punishment depends on the period in which they were brought to answer for their crimes, their age, social class and marital status, as well as the number of previous offences or convictions. There were no hard and fast rules concerning the extent of punishment available for any particular crime. That was usually left to the learned judge to implement, based on his legal training and expertise in sitting in judgement. Some were wrongly convicted, others served harsher sentences than those tried for the same sort of crime while the occasional guilty individual got away scot free. Nothing has changed since then compared to the legal system today. Probably the biggest difference, dependent on the period involved, is the opportunity for the accused to offer their side of the story to the court, giving evidence themselves rather than relying on the eloquence of a lawyer, if they could afford one. The opportunity to appeal against a sentence gives a glimmer of hope for those wrongly accused, or punished more severely than others guilty of a similar offence certainly exists today whereas it was unheard of when some of the events in this book took place. While the death penalty no longer exists for any crime in present times, whatever your personal thoughts on its removal as the ultimate punishment for criminals, the crimes committed by those upon whom it was given were much less serious than murder, manslaughter and treason, the crimes we usually think deserving of it. Whatever punishment was meted out, it makes excellent material for another Taunton Casebook.

Note – Picking oakum was a common task within prisons and workhouses. It involved the dismantling of old rope, usually obtained from ships, by pulling it apart by hand. The piles of oakum would be sold by the institution, and was used to stuff mattresses, or to be wedged between the planking on the hulls of ships (and then tarred to make it waterproof).

IN THE NEWS
Somerset County Gazette: 12 May 1888 edtn:

Taunton Police Court – George Gill, Charles Sparks, Frederick Ware, Samuel Spark and Joseph Marshalsea, small boys living in the Upper High Street neighbourhood, were charged with breaking eleven squares of glass, valued at ten shillings, property of Augustus Chubb of Rowbarton.
Chubb had an empty house in Upper High Street and informed the police when he found upstairs windows broken. P.C. Bourne saw the defendants on April 31st – all except Spark admitted the damage (there was no evidence ahainst Spark, and he was discharged) and were fined sixpence each. Chubb waived his claim for damages and costs were remitted.

Leeds Times: 9 February 1884 edtn:

Taunton Assizes – Mary Ann Lee (39), daughter of a retired farmer of Taunton, sued George Lockyer (53), farmer of Boro'bridge , for breach of promise of marriage.
She entered his service in 1881 as his housekeeper and had full control of his domestic affairs.
The Jury found for the plaintiff, and awarded £125 damages.

Shepton Mallet Journal: 26 October 1888 edtn:

Taunton Police Court – William Lawrence,a packer in the employ of Excelsior Collar Works Co., was sentenced to four months' hard labour for stealing shirts and other articles belonging to his masters.

4. THE GOVIER FAMILY

Most families have a black sheep, or one of a number of differing shades of grey. Usually, it is someone who has stepped into a life of crime and made several appearances in court, suffering the penalties thereof. For some, their crimes made front page headlines, or live to this day in infamy for their deeds. Reserving such accolades for others, the Govier family of Taunton were spotted because one of their number appeared in court, and the case was reported in the *Bristol Times & Mirror (18 Dec 1868 edtn)*:

"Taunton County Court – Miss CATHERINE GOVIER, dressmaker of North Town, Taunton, bankrupt, came up for last examination and discharge. She was engaged to marry a young man in India, who some time since sent her a considerable sum of money to proceed to India for their marriage. She spent a part on an outfit befitting a lady about to be married, and gave up her business. As she was about to leave the country, his letter arrived, saying he had changed his mind, and she need not come. He also wrote to his friends in England and gave them the money he had sent to her. She refused to give it up and they brought an action against her at the last Wells Sessions – The Verdict was against her, with the judge saying she had good grounds for breach of promise against "her gay deceiver". The cost of defending this action was £50 which, with the £20 she lent to her father (who since became bankrupt himself) entirely ruined her. Discharge granted."

Catherine had clearly got herself into financial straits because her fiancé changed his mind, and claimed back the money sent to aid her voyage to join him. His so-called friends made things worse by taking Catherine to court to claim back the cash, which funds she clearly used to defend herself, having already given £20 to her father to help him financially, though to no avail. This all caused her to be declared bankrupt, as her dressmaking business was no more (women about to become wives were not expected to have businesses, nor to continue them after marriage). Whether she pursued the suggested breach of promise matter has not been pursued, but she was certainly of great interest. Just who was her father, the man who subsequently went bankrupt despite his daughter's generosity (£20 in 1868 would compare with an income of about £13,000 in 2020)?

The name of Govier has been appearing in the Taunton records since the late 16th century, though these antecedents need not be related to Catherine and her family. Usually, it is easy to find a candidate for the lady in question but, in this particular matter, there is nothing positive for a Catherine Govier of appropriate age in Taunton to be considering marriage in 1868 (minimum age for a girl was twelve years of age, and fourteen for a male, at this time).
Trying a different tack, a Catholine Govier was employed as a dressmaker at the time of the 1861 census. Knowing the rate of illiteracy in the 19th century, this was somewhere to start at least. It also seems to be in line with notice of her bankruptcy in the autumn of 1868 as Catholine Govier of Taunton, dressmaker.

Catholine was living at home in 1861 with parents Jacob and Elizabeth in Yarde Place, Taunton. Jacob earned his living as a sawyer, and had two further children at home at this time. A requirement of the census was to state where you were born, except not everybody knew where they were born. This leads to information being erratic and erroneous, but on this census, Jacob Govier said he was born in Blagdon. Ten years earlier, he was in the same trade and location with no further changes beyond another child being at home at that time, and daughter Catherine alias Catholine is now written as Caroline. By 1871, Jacob is giving Pitminster as his place of birth, which leads to his baptism in the Fulwood Independent Chapel there in 1815, son of William Govier, a labourer of Pitminster, and his wife Mary. So, was Jacob ever bankrupt?

In 1837, Jacob and Isaac Govier were tried at the County Sessions in Taunton for assaulting one John Hartnell. They were both sawyers by trade, and held in Ilchester Gaol until their trial but were found not guilty. Isaac was one of Jacob's brothers, and they appear to have had a difficult relationship with each other over the years. Already known to be a sawyer, by 1865, Jacob was referred to as a builder on the marriage lines of his daughter, Eliza Drousilla, to printer Charles Lilley Parkhouse.
In 1864, Jacob the builder fell foul of rules and regulations imposed on the building of new structures in Taunton. He was fined £1 for the offence of erecting of a house in Wood Street on the Yard Estate

without depositing the proper plans with the Taunton Board of Health, who oversaw such work at that time. He was fined a further £1 for building a house and permitting it to be occupied without certification that the property was fit for human habitation, and yet another £1 for building on what should have been left as an open space for the health of the residents, as indicated and approved on some previous plans. He was about to build another two houses in Wood Street but those plans had already been approved, and afterwards that construction was deemed habitable and accordingly occupied.

It appears that his desire to build on that designated open space was only discovered by a diligent official who told the enquiry that the place was somewhat hidden from the street and difficult to find. During his visit, the official noted that it was already in the occupation of a woman named Thorn with her child and she had been living there for six weeks.

Four years on from these fines and Jacob was in financial trouble to such an extent that he appears on the list of bankrupts for 5 Sep 1868 as a timber merchant in Taunton. He was up in Taunton County Court as a timber merchant of Taunton and Tiverton for his last examination and discharge in bankruptcy, owing £156.0s.4d to unsecured creditors with assets of only £5-14s-6d. This appears to have taken place soon after his daughter, Catherine, faced bankruptcy herself.

A third Govier was pronounced a bankrupt in the same season of 1868 – Isaac Govier, Jacob's brother, and uncle to the said Catherine or Catholine the dressmaker. Isaac appears to have been on the edge of bankruptcy in 1864 as well, when notice of impending proceedings referred to him as an innkeeper and timber and hay dealer of Alma Street, Taunton, and late a prisoner for debt in the Somerset County Prison at Taunton. The 1864 edition of the Taunton street directory indicates Isaac to have been the landlord of the Alma Inn.

In 1869, Jacob Govier charged his brother, Isaac, with the theft of a chain from a timber carriage that Jacob owned. Valued to be worth five shillings, he noticed the chain was missing when his timber carriage was at the railway station, and the said item was later found in Isaac's yard. No exact details were printed in the local papers but somehow it was judged that the chain was actually Isaac's property in the first place, and the case was dismissed "to the evident satisfaction of the people in the court" as the *Western Gazette* put it (7 May 1869 edition) and "admidst the congratulations of the people in the court" according to the reporter for the *Taunton Courier & Western Advertiser (*5 May 1869 edtn*)*.

In the following edition of the *Western Gazette* (14 May), there was more about the two brothers and their situation.

Isaac was accused of stealing a horse from his brother, for which he was duly discharged, but more information about their respective bankruptcies was given. Isaac had got into financial difficulties "some time ago" and the horse and a timber carriage went into Jacob's possession. Isaac claimed Jacob had bought them. Isaac then went through the proceedings of bankruptcy, and brother Jacob followed suit. It became necessary for Jacob to sell the same horse and carriage, goods for which he had been an assignee under the terms of Isaac's bankruptcy case, and he had sold them to his (Jacob's) son. When Jacob passed through the court, Isaac claimed that he had purchased the said items back again from Jacob's son and therefore laid claim to them as his own property. In the darkness of night, Isaac went to his brother's premises and retrieved them, taking them back to his own establishment, hence Jacob's action for their return. Mr Cook, solicitor, then put in a claim on the said items on behalf of Isaac's creditors, to offset his debts under the order of bankruptcy. This led to the judge questioning whether Jacob Govier had been guilty of fraud for his actions as Isaac's assignee in bankruptcy. The case was adjourned, and- as yet – no verdict has been considered further.

The *Western Gazette* also reported alongside the above article a snippet that Henry Walter Govier had pleaded guilty to assaulting his cousin, William Govier, for which he was fined ten shillings with costs. Henry was Jacob's son, then 22 years of age.

This was not Henry's first appearance in court for assault. In 1866, he was summoned by Robert Davey for assaulting him on November 3rd. Davey resided with his aunt, Mrs Loader, in Wood Street, Taunton, and their home must have belonged to the Govier family. Henry was sent by his father (Jacob) to nail up the door to an outbuilding. Davey seemed to think Henry was going to nail him up inside their property and there was the typical sort of verbal confrontation between them before Henry struck Davey a blow in his left eye, followed by another to the right and a third to the chest. Davey went for the police. Henry said he did not strike Davey first as he had been the object of a punch that failed to land squarely upon him, and he had struck out in retaliation. The witnesses to this little fracas included Mrs Mary Govier, another aunt to Robert Davey (and also cousin to the said Henry), and her niece, Jane Brown. A counter-summons was issued by Henry against Robert Davey that he, Davey, had been the first to make an assault and that Henry had only returned the blows. There does not appear to have been a firm picture of what happened from any of the witnesses and, after Henry's father, Jacob Govier, had been called to give his evidence (presumably that he had authorised Henry to nail up the door to the outbuilding), both summonses were dismissed by the court.

Jacob Govier, Catholine's father, was not always the perpetrator; on one occasion he was the targeted victim of a female named Emma Harvey. She was described as "a miserable specimen of the Taunton *Demi-monde*" when she was charged with stealing five half-sovereigns, a half-crown and a florin from the person of Jacob Govier, timber merchant of Wood Street, Taunton. Govier made her acquaintance, and that of "her man", William Palfrey (who was also charged with receiving the said coins), at the Swan Inn, Kingston, where Govier treated her to two glasses of brandy and water. He then offered her a ride on the back of his horse while Palfrey walked alongside. Whilst riding, Jacob claimed he felt her hands in his pockets and then discovered he had been robbed. He said he saw her hand something to Palfrey but he and Harvey both denied doing anything. Jacob then accused both of them of theft, and again they denied it. He even offered them five shillings to return his missing money, along with his promise not to fetch the police, but they denied they had taken anything from him. Govier fetched the law. While at the Swan Inn, Govier was known to have paid for a glass of "rum & shrub*" for the landlady, a glass of brandy and water for the servant there, as well as half a gallon of beer and a quartern of brandy for Palfrey, something Govier said was for Palfrey to carry home so he could whet his whistle when he returned from the Traveller's Rest, which is where he (Govier) was heading. The police commented that Jacob Govier was very tipsy and the two accused had only a few pennies between them. It was decided that the matter was too doubtful to be pursued, and Harvey and Palfrey were discharged.

The Govier family seem to have migrated into Taunton from Pitminster, and a number of brothers worked as sawyers, or an allied trade in the town. As well as being involved in the timber trade, several members of this family became innkeepers in the town.

There are more court appearances for others named Govier in Taunton, and in Somerset, should anyone wish to follow them further. They just show that Victorian law was hard on the poorer classes, especially when they showed signs of drinking heavily, squabbling with each other and bending the law when trying to better themselves. Wish we could speak with them today … what a tale they might tell!

*Shrub was a popular dark rum-based liqeur, flavoured with citrus and ginger, that was very much a lady's tipple, either neat or as a cocktail. The flavouring was developed from the time when rum was smuggled into the country in barrels. The barrels often spent time anchored at sea, which left the liquor with a slightly brackish taste. Its saltiness was disguised with the additional sweetness and spices. It became a popular drink in Cornwall, home to many smugglers and their families.

5. THE TAUNTON BIGAMY CASE

A few details of what was entitled "The Taunton Bigamy Case" were found in the *Western Somerset Free Press (28 Aug 1886 edtn).*

In the dock was 28 year old Henry James Clark, described as "a well-dressed young man", for entering into marriage with one Annie Philpott on June 5th 1880 while his legal wife was still alive.
The case was heard in the Westminster Police Court, and Clarke or Clark had been carrying on a business as a baker and confectioner at 105 High Street, Ventnor, Isle of Wight until his arrest. A writ of *Habeus Corpus* was instigated because he was in custody for abduction at the time of the bigamy trial, and therefore appeared between two warders from Holloway Gaol. Known for being the women's prison that finally closed in 2016, and where many of the suffragettes were incarcerated, it became a female-only gaol in 1903. Therefore, Clarke spent time there while it catered for both sexes from 1852.

With no legal representation to speak on his behalf, Clarke had been charged with abducting a female named Kate Hardwick who had been placed into the care of Clarke and his wife at Ventnor by the girl's parents. Kate was not yet sixteen years of age, and she was to learn the trade of a pastrycook from the Clarkes, and become efficient in all aspects of running a confectionary business. When giving her evidence to the court, Kate claimed that Clarke had forced his way into her bedroom whilst his wife was absent from the premises. Details of what happened were not given … or not reported … but the pair of them – Clarke and the girl - then eloped, finding their way to London where they lived together as man and wife at a house in Chelsea for several weeks. The legal age for marriage for a female at the time of this offence was twelve years of age (and fourteen as a minimum for males), so it seems somewhat out of place for the period to consider the girl as being abducted – a term that suggests she was taken somewhere against her will.
There is little reported about what subsequently happened after they fled to London, but Clarke gets arrested in Bognor Regis, Sussex, and was sent to Holloway to await trial.

His brush with bigamy then comes into the arena, and some newspapers give more details of the two marriages rather than information of his relationship with young Kate. Reporters in 1886 were clearly uncertain what to write, or even how to be accurate, as you will now see.

It was reported at trial that Clarke started to pay attention to a female named Annie Scuse in 1879, and he was said to then be "of Ely, near Taunton". There is certainly an Ely in Cambridgeshire, known for its cathedral, but nowhere of the same name has been located in Somerset. Perhaps Clarke was visiting Taunton from Ely when he became acquainted with the woman to whom he was married on August 5th 1878 at Ely, Cambs. Using "James Clarke" as his name, he was then a clerk living in Church Lane in Ely, and his father was identified as William Clarke, a harness-maker. Annie, whose surname is sometimes written as "Scrase", was emploted as a domestic servant in Church Lane (probably how they met originally) and her father is given as Alfred, a carpenter. In evidence, Clarke's sister, Mrs Annie Berry of 19 Chelsea Park Dwellings, Chelsea, stated that she had been present at this ceremony, which took place in St Mary's schoolroom in Ely and her brother had used "James Clarke" as his name. When asked if he had any questions for his sister, Clarke replied in the negative.

Next to give evidence was the bigamous wife, Annie Philpott. She was resident at 1 Holland Park Road, Kensington at this time and said that she went to live in Taunton in the spring of 1880. She met Clarke there while he was employed as a baker and pastrycook at the Wesleyan College in the town. Thye started to get acquainted with each other. He never told her that he was married, so she claimed, but he hadn't indicated he was free to marry either. Annie simply assumed from his attentions that he was a bachelor. They were married at Taunton Wesleyan Chapel in June of that same year, not very long after they first met. Annie told the court that they became husband and wife only four months after their first meeting. When interrogated about this second wedding, Clarke did not answer. He did ask if he could pose a question to his sister but, when granted, decided to keep that option for his trial. The matter was duly referred to the Central Criminal Court, or, as we generally call it today The Old Bailey (though the former is the official title), and Clarke returned to Holloway with his escorts in a handsome cab.

Records of the Old Bailey cases are available online, though not every case is fully covered in its entirety. Some details are simply given as a series of short sentences … as is the case in the matters relating to Henry James Clarke. Again, his sister Annie (now described as the wife of Alfred Bury – note the alternate spelling of her surname) and the bigamous wife, Annie, have their evidence documented in a series of short statements. On this occasion, his sister mentions that Mrs Clarke is present, presumably referring to his legal wife, also called Annie, nee Scuse, Scruse or Scrase, but this legal spouse does not appear to have given any evidence.

According to the *West Somerset Free Press (18 Sep 1886 edtn)*, Clarke was found guilty of an assault at London on Kate Howick (when she was under 16 years of age) and he was duly sentenced to two years imprisonment with hard labour. In the Old Bailey's record, he was found guilty and so sentenced for "carnal knowledge of the said girl". The quoted publication added that the bigamy charge was not taken (probably meaning not included) but the court records show he received a further two year sentence for that infringement of the law. It does not say if the two sentences were to run consecutively or concurrently, but he went into Pentonville Prison to serve the two year term required.

Reports of the case appeared in newspapers all across the country but they all seem to run along the same lines of text. Perhaps one enterprising reporter managed to sell his article to several papers or, more likely, each newspaper sold it on to another. The Isle of Wight local paper gives some extra detail just prior to Clarke's appearance in the Old Bailey. It added Kate Howick was the daughter of a publican at Bognor, and that Clark – that's how they spelled his surname – was managing a baker's shop in Ventnor. That seems more likely, given he was a clerk in 1878, rather than he retrained in the art of baking after marrying Annie Scruse, or Leruse as the same paper printed his first wife's maiden name, though that could be the result of sloppy type-setting or appalling handwriting. It identified Clarke's sister as the wife of a painter who was living just off the King's Road in Kensington. There was also a small scrap of information that Annie Philpott was in Taunton in 1880 and staying with her parents. While one newspaper report showed Clarke requested to question his sister and then reserved that right for his trial, the Isle of Wight publication directed his question request was to be put to his first wife – about whom nothing is ever included beyond her name and the date of that marriage. The supposed bigamous wife appears to have asked the Central Criminal Court to understand that she did not wish to punish him, and that he was "a very good husband" to her. Nothing has been located concerning any part of the first marriage, or questions put to Annie Scruse about it, but in the legal argument and subsequent summing up it appears that there was no evidence (beyond the actual certificate produced in evidence as Exhibit A) that his first marriage was actually legal. That decision was left to the Jury sitting listening to this plethora of confusing information, and they must have decided the legality of the 1878 marriage in Ely because they found him guilty of bigamy.

With so many names, it should be relatively easy to locate more information about the participants in this drama. Howick seems the most unusual but there is nothing standing out on the 1871, 1881 or 1891 census returns for a Kate who would be under 16 years old in 1886. The most likely candidate was recorded on the 1881 census as a ten year old (born about 1871 and therefore around 15 when she was mixed up with Clarke) and was living with publican father Henry Howick at 71 High Street, Bognor. The property is named as the Fountain Inn and the family were local to the town.
Things are far more difficult for Henry … or should that be James … Clarke, or Clark, on the quoted census records; no clues for an Annie Clarke or Clark marrying an Alfred Berry or Bury, and neither of them on the 1881 or 1891 census. Nothing is forthcoming for an Annie Philpott on the quoted records and it is presumed she just picked up her single life again after 1886. There are just too many possibilities that she married a legal husband, and no idea whether she came back to Taunton or remained in London.

And what of the wronged legal first wife? Where was she in 1881, or 1891? With the surname of Clark, or perhaps Clarke, and such a common first name, she could be anywhere and there are too many possibilities to chase further for this book. It is the same with the man she married – lots of possibilities but with only an approximate year of birth of 1859 and no location for that event, he remains the mystery he was before the newspapers started to publish the details of his peccadillos in the late 19th century.

6. THE PYRLAND HALL BURGLARY

Being a newcomer to Taunton, now a resident for some years, one of the first things on a "to do" list was to join the library and find out about the town's history. In a book on the shelves of the Somerset Heritage Centre, the tale of the Pyrland Hall Burglary was discovered (*"Taunton A to Z"* by Lionel Ward; published 2008).

The account stated that a gang broke into the Hall and tied up Sir William Yea, the owner-occupier at the time, but he managed to escape and the thieves left empty-handed. The gang's leader was given as one Thomas Gage, who was subsequently executed for the crime at Dodhill Green. No date was recorded in this rendition beyond the year – 1793. It noted that, with the assistance of the housekeeper at the Hall, aided by a page – with whom she is later supposed to have run away to Jersey in the Channel Islands and got married - five or six individuals were allowed to enter the property around midnight, with the intention of robbing it. Their faces draped in black crape, they found the owner, Sir William Yea, and his nephew at supper in the dining room. It might help to mention that in the Georgian era, it was commonplace to eat the final meal of the day as late as ten, eleven, even twelve o'clock at night so finding the two men at the dinig table despite it being near midnight would not have raised eyebrows … except for the two men surprised by their uninvited visitors.
The nephew was not expected to be present but had returned from his travels unexpectedly and, as the thieves entered, he leapt out through the window to make his escape. The windows of the dining room at Pyrland Hall are tall and the sills are close to the ground, making a desperate jump through one of them an easy exercise, providing they had been opened first of course. The nephew then proceeded to run the two miles into Taunton to get help, without street lighting and likely without a flaming torch either. He would probably have travelled along what is now the Kingston Road, and the main drive from Pyrland Hall is though to have originally been accessible around the junction of Hope Corner Lane, Corkscrew Lane and the said road, or perhaps he opted to follow what is now Cheddon Road. Either route may have been nothing more than a well-used track, not the metalled surface we are familiar with today, but they could have been as

peppered with pot-holes from coaches and carts as our roads are today from bad weather.

Continuing with Ward's version of events, the thieves tied Sir William into his chair, using some cord they brought with them, which restraints resembled that used by shoemakers at that time. They then went off around the rooms of the hall looking for suitable loot. Left alone, Sir William managed to drag his chair to the table, where a large carving knife lay. He somehow managed to take hold of this weapon, using it to cut himself free of his bonds, and then wielding it to keep the raiders at bay while he awaited help from the town. It is said that he waited an hour for some form of assistance to arrive. Either as the nephew returned with suitable strong-armed men , or prior to their appearance at the Hall, the thieves ran off, apparently taking nothing at all. If this was the case, not only were they very ineffective robbers, but how could they be tracked down if they had donned some form of disguise? Never mind the fact that Gage appears to have paid with his life for a crime that left Sir William Yea with all his wealth anyway – unless they saw that as "breaking and entering". If this account is correct, the robbers never even broke in but walked through an open door, courtesy of the Hall's domestic staff.

Eventually, the ringleader of this non-burglary was tracked down and taken to trial, where a shoemaker from Taunton town told the court that he had sold a ball of cord a few days before the burglary to someone who lived close to Pyrland Hall. With such evidence, the leader of this thieving bunch – who was said in the quoted volume to be a resident in Nailsbourne in the parish of Kingston St Mary – was found guilty and sentenced to death.

The usual punishment was hanging, and it took place at Dodhill Green, which also lies within Kingston parish and is just a short ride across the field from Pyrland Hall. Thousands of locals supposedly flocked to watch the spectacle, including Sir William himself, and it is said that he ordered the body to be turned around so all present could see the face of the condemned man in order to reflect on his fate. This all sounds typical for the late 18th century except ... no record of any hangings for burglary have come to light in 1793, certainly none at Dodhill Green, and nothing in Somerset for the burial of a Thomas Gage. Would a man be hanged for a burglary where nothing was taken? Making an example of him for the audacity of committing the burglary, especially on the mansion of a prominent citizen of the county, would more likely be some form of imprisonment with the possibility of a public flogging or time in the stocks or pillory. There is also a question regarding the numbers of spectators for the grisly execution – could Dodhill Green have accommodated thousands? Where would these thousands of rubber-neckers have actually come from? Was Taunton and the surrounding area able to sustain thousands of people in 1793, either as residents or as visitors?

In trying to found out more about Gage and his role in the burglary of 1793, another name came forward, connected to a Pyrland Hall Burglary in 1788 – Samuel Yendall. He was definitely a tenant of Sir William Yea, and he leased property in Nailsbourne.

Under some information in the 1942 copy of the local newspaper for Taunton relating to the history of Nailsbourne, another account of the same burglary refers back to the event taking place in 1793 and that the ringleader of four or five men came from there. In that particular account, the gang gained access to the building with the connivance of two dishonest servants. With faces masked by black crape, they seized Sir William Yea and his nephew while the two men were partaking of supper, and the younger man jumped out of the window and ran to Taunton for assistance. Meanwhile, Sir William was tied up while the thieves ransacked his home. Sir William managed to get to a carving knife, with which he cut his fetters and defended himself for over an hour against the ruffians. Eventually his assailants departed but were tracked down, their leader being located hiding in the roof of his Nailsbourne home. He was tried, found guilty, and executed at Dodhill Green in front of a crowd numbering thousands. Sir William Yea on horseback, and wearing the uniform of deputy lieutenant of the county, rode out from Pyrland Hall at the head of his servants to see justice being done.

Many of the above details reflect those in Ward's book – two servants (presumably housekeeper and page), the black crape, Sir William being tied up, freeing himself by means of a knife and then holding the intruders at bay, a nephew visiting the Hall – but no mention of a Thomas Gage in this account. Beyond Sir William, no names had been committed to paper.

In *Salisbury & Winchester Journal* (Monday 18th Feb 1788 edtn; page

3), a report of the event by someone who heard of it first hand was printed. This time, the intrusion occurred on a Friday evening, on February the 8th of that year, when two ruffians with blackened faces forced their way into Pyrland Hall armed with bludgeons. They threatened the occupant, Sir William Yea, after knocking down George Yea (Sir William's son) and a female servant. George Yea recovered almost immediately and attacked the villains, tearing part of a waistcoat worn by one of them, wrenching a pistol from the other and causing both intruders to run off. Does this mean George was dining with his father on the night in question as well as Sir William's nephew, or has the word "nephew" taken the place of "son"? Certainly none of the accounts name Sir William's dining companion. What happened about somebody – be it nephew or son - running off to get help, and where is the knife that appeared in the version attributed to 1793? Or the cords that tied Sir William to the chair in that same year for that matter?

Those cords did get a mention in the article, but now numbering a dozen such items that had been brought to tie up members of the family whilst the burglars robbed the house. It was reported in the 1788 burglary account that these restraints had been left behind, along with a hat and one of the bludgeons, when the burglars ran off. Through those discarded items, the perpetrators were finally tracked down but before following that clue, this contemporary article of 1788 stated that they, the intruders, probably hoped to find cash to help themselves to, as rumours suggested Sir William kept plenty close at hand. One small sentence also raises an eyebrow …"*The house was robbed about two years since of a quantity of plate.*" Had there been a number of burglaries at Sir William Yea's home over a number of years, to such an extent that the accounts of each one have become merged into a complicated but inaccurate account?

The mansion known as Pyrland Hall was built by Sir William Yea in 1760 to reflect his position in society as a baronet, and as a suitable domicile for the lieutenant for Somerset. Today, it is a school.
It is only natural that Yea would have furnished it in a grand style, complete with beautiful – and expensive – items, and that such obvious wealth would be talked about, gossiped about and plans made to obtain it. However, the 1788 account mentions only two robbers with faces blackened, not a gang of four, five or six men with their faces swathed in black crape – though you could argue it might be the

same thing - while the numbers being increased could have happened with constant exaggeration in retelling the tale. The same article also adds that information " ... has since been made of two very suspicious fellows who are apprehended, lately from London, where they worked as sawyers; the hat is known to belong to one of them, also the waistcoat ..." So, in the earlier burglary (1788), the authorities had two men in custody, which individuals had lately been employed in London as sawyers (preparers of wood and timber), and to whom belonged the hat and waistcoat piece that were left behind when the miscreants fled.

The 1788 version seems to be virtually the same as that credited to 1793, but without embellishments of the servants, numbers of burglars, the dining room, etc. That isn't to say those things didn't occur, only that no mention was made of such detail in 1788.

From newspapers of the day, it appears that Pyrland House, as the Hall was frequently known then, and its estate was subject to a series of petty thefts of deer, sheep, fowls and wool in varying degrees and on different occasions. As a whole, the stolen goods came to a substantial amount and clearly Sir William would be very concerned, especially if the culprit or culprits could not be determined. The stolen goods seem to have been sold or destroyed, as none get reported as having been found and returned, or maybe such positive results weren't deemed newsworthy.

It was put forward that the 1788 burglary had been concocted by two men from Brompton Ralph, along with an accomplice who came with from London. The timing of the burglary is also unclear as "supper" was often a late night repast, sometimes as late as midnight. The nephew and the son might be one and the same, and, perhaps, after his encounter with the burglars, the son runs off for help, probably realising there are too many for him and his father keep at bay and that someone needs to raise the alarm. After securing Sir William, maybe only two burglars were within his eyesight and, once he managed to free himself - due to their inattention to his circumstances - he goes for them, causing one ... or both ... to bolt.

The fact that the ringleader is said to have been found hiding in the roof space of his (the burglar's) house at Nailsbourne during an intense search of that particular settlement does tend to imply that someone might have been recognised by Sir William at the time. Otherwise, why choose Nailsbourne as the most likely place to find the miscreants, regardless of the number involved? The burglar only revealed himself after a spit (a thin metal rod) was thrust into the thatch of the roof.

These events led to Samuel Yendall being tried at the Spring Assizes held in 1788 in Taunton, charged under the "Black Act" with cutting and wounding Sir William Yea, baronet. Hang on! No account has mentioned any form of injury to Sir William's person, or to his son/nephew for that matter, though one newspaper did say that Sir William had been "violently assaulted" during a burglary but it was printing information about Yendall's execution at the time.

The Black Act 1723 was a national response to a series of raids by two groups of poachers known as The Blacks. Over the years, it was expanded, and greatly strengthened the criminal code. It listed over 200 capital crimes, such as the offence of arson being increased to include the threat of burning haystacks as well as the actual act. Defendants found their rights limited by this legislation, such as suspects who refused to surrender within forty days of an offence would be judged to be guilty and sentenced to be executed once taken up. Local villages were also subject to punishment if they failed to find such suspects, thus explaining the search of Nailsbourne mentioned before.

Yendall appeared at the Somerset Assizes along with a John Yendall and a Betty Yendall. Whilst Samuel was charged with the burglary and violent assaults on Sir William and his son, the said John & Betty were charged with aiding and abetting the alleged assault on Sir William. This suggests that not only could they be related to Samuel but that they were both present at Pyrland Hall and participated in the actual burglary in some way. Betty can be identified as Samuel's wife and was probably expecting twins at the time. Samuel's father was named John Yendall, and he also had a brother of the same name, either of whom could have been the co-accused with Betty. The brother sems a better bet because a younger man would be more agile if escape and flight became necessary.

Tried at the same sessions was James Sayer, for stealing sheep and deer from Sir William, along with James Shallis for the same offence. Could these be two more of the alleged "gang" that implemented the 1788 burglary? Have these details become confused with a copycat burglary in 1793?

There was quoted suspicion that these two men were the London connection hinted at in regard to the abandoned hat and the torn waistcoat. A James Shallis was baptised in the Somerset parish of Brompton Ralph in 1747, and married there in 1780.

All four of the co-accused mentioned here - Sayer, Shallis and the other two Yendalls - were acquitted, leaving only Samuel Yendall to pay the price for the crime. His sentence was to take place within a few days of the trial and the place was designated as "opposite Sir William's house". Dodhill Green would fit the bill, though not fully visible from Pyrland Hall due to the trees planted to keep Yea's mansion as private as possible. It does however also fit with Yendall being executed in a place where his family and neighbours could witness his end, as a lesson of where such criminal acts could lead. His corpse was probably left hanging for several days.

Yendall's demise warranted a mention in *Northampton Mercury (19 April 1788 edtn)* as his execution, with others, was reported:

TAUNTON – April 11 – Yesterday, John Lewis, condemned at the last Assizes for horse-stealing, was executed at Stone Gallows: and SAMUEL YENDALL, for burglary and assault at Sir W Yea's, was executed at Deadman's Green, on a Gibbet 20 feet high. They did not make a confession. Yendall rented an estate of Sir William, near the place where he was executed.

These few sentences shed a new light on the situation. Yendall is now recorded as being found guilty of burglary and assault, yet no newspaper had made any mention of any physical injury made on Sir William's person. This extra "charge" may simply be the result of the phrase "charged under the Black Act", and any bodily harm would be implied by it.

Whilst nothing has been located about a hanging at any time in a place called Deadman's Green – unless this is an error for Dodhill Green - it has been discovered that Yendall rented property from Sir William Yea, and an indenture dated 28 January 1789 confirms this. It was between the said Sir William Yea and one Richard Richards of Rapsile in the parish of Taunton St James, yeoman, and concerned two properties. The first was in Rapsile and had previously been in the hands of one John Chick as the tenant, and the other was "a messuage in Nailesbourne with several closes, late in the occupation of William Harris, and since of Samuel Yandell, tenant of Sir William Yea, now of Richard Richards – with all houses, outhouses, barns, buildings, curtilages, yards gardens, orchards, lands, ways, paths, watercourses, etc., belonging to the same …". It sounds like a substantial property, but some of the terms used were included to cover all types of buildings and hovels, even if they didn't actually exist. Yea had originally leased the property to someone named William Harris, and then to Samuel Yendall, but the latter was no longer in possession of it by early 1789 when it was passed into the tenure of Richard Richards. It dovetails very neatly with Samuel's execution in 1788, at which point his wife and family would have been ejected from their home by Yea.

Sir William Yea was created a baronet on 18 June 1759, and about the same time, with his wife, Julia (daughter of Sir George Trevelyan, 3rd baronet), purchased a copyhold property belonging to the Manor of Taunton Deane and known as Pyrland, on which they set about building their home. They shared their building with Julia's brother, (Sir) John Trevelyan for a while. There may have been a building on the property when it was acquired by the couple, and there is an old structure still standing at the Cheddon Road entrance to the present Pyrland Hall.

The Yea family can be traced back to the late 15th century in Wiveliscombe. In 1760, Sir William served as the High Sheriff of Somerset, and was also a Justice of the Peace for the county. His descendants could, through Julia Trevelyan's ancestry, claim descent from King Edward III of England and Queen Philippa (of Hainault) through two separate lines – one side from an illegitimate line descending from John of Gaunt (died 1399) and his mistress/wife, Catherine, and the other through John's younger brother, Thomas of Woodstock, Duke of Gloucester. Their great-grandchildren married to form a direct link to Sir William Yea's children, but this digresses from the subject in hand.

Sir William was soon a wealthy landowner. He does not appear to have been a benevolent landlord, nor a law-abiding one. In 1779, he was tried at Bridgwater Assizes on three charges; two for forcible entry and a third for "a very outrageous assault on his tenant's wife". Yandell was not a married man in 1779 (he marries Betty Robert in Taunton in 1785) but he and his family had lived in and around Nailsbourne for a couple of decades and more. Did Samuel know the assaulted wife? Did Sir William's attitude towards his tenants and their families colour Samuel's actions, or was it the impending birth of Samuel's child (the twins he never saw) that made a burglary necessary?

Sir William received a fine of £140 (the equivalent in 2020 would be earning over £19,000 in a year) and two months' imprisonment for the quoted offences. In 1786, he was facing the Dean & Chapter of Wells for an action of trespass against them, which he lost, while in 1793, he was charged with selling four eggs at a cost of four guineas. Hhhmmm … that's the same year as the supposed burglary alleged to have been led by Thomas Gage.

And what of the Yendall family? Betty baptised twin sons James and Samuel at Kingston St Mary on the first day of September 1788, five months after their father's execution. She would have lost her home at Nailsbourne almost as he was arrested. She could have been taken in by his family, which would explain the baptism of her twins there, and then probably went back to live with her own family in Taunton, where she married a second time after Christmas 1790 to John Hoare Davy. There was one child, a son, from her second marriage, whose only child, Betty's grandson, died in infancy. Poor Betty lost her first son, Ardeman Roberts Yendall in his first year of life, and twin son Samuel was buried six weeks after baptism. The other twin, James Yendall (1788-1834) survived to marry and fathered six children before being buried at Kingston.

His father would not have received such a ceremony. As a felon, he would have been buried somewhere near to the 20 foot high gibbet on which his life ended – unmarked and unknown, except for uncovering the reason for his disappearance. This might be of interest to his descendants, of which there could still be living members.

Descendants can be traced to the Weston-Super-Mare area in the last quarter of the 20th century. Not only could they claim Samuel Yendall in their pedigree – though not everyone is proud of having an executed felon in the ancestry – perhaps their family stories could explain why the 1788 burglary at Pyrland Hall has somehow been mashed together with another such incident in 1793. Just as Samuel Yendall has faded into history, so has his nemesis, Sir William Yea, whose descendants sold the Hall.

A final note of irony; whilst Sir William Yea lived in splendour in his mansion, Pyrland Hall, his distant relatives were living in Kingston St Mary, the parish that adjoined the Pyrland estate. One wonders if they were aware of the relationship or whether it was long forgotten. Sir William descended through the Yea line that was settled in Wiveliscombe by 1500, and where his grandfather, David Yea, was a brewer and also held office as a sheriff of the county of Somerset. The said David Yea was responsible for building Oakhampton Manor in Wiveliscombe parish in 1734 but the building was utterly destroyed by fire in 1956. Sir William was baptised in 1727 in the parish church of Brompton Ralph – a parish that featured in the case against Samuel Yendall.

Whilst Sir William resided in Pyrland, his distant kinsman, Simon Yea (1699-1782) was settled in Kingston St Mary, probably in the cottage that was known as Yawe's Tenement, a thatched property once held by his grandfather, Robert Yeaw (died 1709, a yeoman) and within which remains the initials "R.Y." and the date "1673", possibly an indication of who built it and when. On a sadder note, the same Simon Yea (1699-1782) had a grandson named William Yea who died on 25th of June 1836, just six days before the introduction of death certificates in England and Wales. He was 65 years of age and drew his last breath in the Dodhill Green Poorhouse – possibly near where Samuel Yendall had drawn his.

Most parishes had poorhouses prior to 1834 when the big union workhouses became more popular. The idea of a poor house – sometimes called Parish Houses or Town Houses – was to look after those who needed support because of unemployment, illness, frailty, age or disability, by offering a meal in return for labour. They didn't always require the paupers to sleep in the poorhouse, as the later union workhouses did.

These smaller establishments were run by a parish, such as Kingston St Mary near Taunton, until it became an economic burden. The law regarding paupers was changed in 1834 to create workhouses that served a number of parishes, and each parish would contribute funds towards it, based on the number of inhabitants in their settlement. Kingston St Mary actually managed two poorhouses – one near the church, the other at Dodhill Green, and both were put up for sale in 1839.

The union workhouses held their own into the 20th century, and were abolished in 1929 but continued under the guise of Public Assistance Institutions (doing more or less the same role as a workhouse) until the introduction of the Welfare State after the Second World War. Many of the edifices that had once carried the name of "workhouse" were still intact, and became suitable for other uses, especially as geriatric and fever hospitals. This gave rise to many elderly individuals refusing to enter such establishments because of the tales they remembered, or had heard from older relatives, about life inside its wall as a pauper. This is what makes history so fascinating but let's stick to the subject in hand – criminal cases with connections to Taunton.

There is still one single thread that needs to be dealt with – Thomas Gage. He certainly was executed but not for burglary. In 1810, he was one of 14 prisoners sentenced to death at the Somerset Assizes and one of four to finally be executed (the others had their sentence commuted) but his crime was murder and robbery. Aged only 18 years, and sometimes known as Thomas Torr, he was employed at Goathurst, near Bridgewater, by a Mr Stering, a small farmer (that's small by the size of his farm, not small as in height). During his employer's absence, he appears to have attempted to rob the Sterings' home and murdered Mrs Sarah Stering either before or during the robbery. In court, the claim was made that Gage attacked Sarah with a hatchet, striking her on the back of the head, and then robbed the house before running off to his father's home at Kingsbrompton where he was arrested.

In his defence, Thomas Gage claimed that he had been involved with the loss of a mare that had belonged to Mrs Stering's father and thought he would be sent to gaol for it, especially when he spotted two men coming towards his master's house. He deduced they were coming for him, and that perempted his actions, which resulted in the murder. At his trial, Gage described these two men, saying they were responsible for the killing, but eventually admitted he had made them up. He then tried to blame another labourer working on the farm, a man name Bryant, but that poor soul was able to prove that he had been sowing wheat at the time of the poor woman's awful death. Eventually, Gage broke down and confessed to what he had done.

His callous actions at such a young age, and the enormity of the crime, made it easy for the jury to find him guilty, and the judge to pronounce the death sentence upon him. He was duly hanged and, like many executed felons at the time, his body was delivered to a surgeon for dissection. This was not so much a further punishment, that could even result in there being no burial for the executed felon, but a way of finding cadavers for surgeons to learn their skills. A shortage of suitable bodies led to an Act of Parliament in 1752 whereby executions could provide suitable corpses. Still there was more required, and soon there was a roaring trade providing the newly dead to medical establishments, even if it meant opening newly buried coffins. Less than twenty years later, the Burke and Hare murders brought this terrible business of the resurrectionists to the forefront. The Government's response was to allow the bodies of those deemed to be paupers who passed away in workhouses to be used for medical instruction as well as those fresh from the gallows. Not that this stopped the body-snatchers, but the call for fresh cadavers slowed to virtually nil by 1844, though there was one isolated case noted in Sheffield in 1862.

7. FRED RIPLEY & ANNIE ROWSELL

It is Boxing Day 1882, a wet day with lots of drizzle, and folk were out and about in the evening, still celebrating Christmas. Business in the Crown & Tower Inn at 43 Silver Street was a little busier than normal for the small alehouse but many of its patrons were regulars. This establishment was then in the hands of Richard and Catherine Lawrence, a couple with local roots, who probably went into the licensed trade after Richard finished his service as a seaman. About 9.30pm, Annie Rowsell, known as Nance, entered the house in the company of one Richard Russell.

It is difficult to decide if Annie and Russell were a couple in the modern sense of the word at this time, or simply two close friends sharing a drink. It is even possible that they had an association that may have been born out of dubious dallyings with a customer. The media of the day were equally uncertain about the two of them – some publications saying they were an item while others were particularly vague about their relationship. It has been discovered that Richard Russell was certainly a widower by 1881, at which time he was living at Holway, Taunton, with his son, David, and working as a general labourer.

Annie & Russell settled themselves in the "front room" of the Crown & Tower – a description that suggests the inn had once been a private house, and very little had taken place in regard to alterations to provide patrons with large open areas to congregate, such as are fairly commonplace in our modern hostelries. In her evidence to the court, inn servant Helen Petherick described the property – " … *the door of the inn opened into a passage, and there was a door on the right hand side of the passage, entering from the street: it was called the front room. The door of that apartment was close to the street. On the left hand side was the kitchen, and beyond that the bar…"*. Already in the front room were two females – Mrs Elizabeth Hodge and Selina Warren, widow – and possibly others.

Roughly fifteen minutes later, Fred Ripley entered. He went into the kitchen and requested of the landlady a pint of half-and-half (half bitter and half mild ale). Mrs Lawrence served him, and gave it to him as a Christmas box. This does imply that he was something of a regular drinker at the inn, or was personally known to the landlady, except it was apparently a custom in the town to give away beer at public houses on Boxing Day. He drank up and left but returned sometime after 10.30pm. This return visit goes well with the concept that he was regular customer, and he probably lived nearby. In court, it was stated that he lived with his grandmother who ran a small shop on East Reach but he is not listed there on the 1881 census. However, his youngest sister, Emily Ripley, was living with this said grandmother, Sarah Brown, widow, at 158 East Reach when the 1881 census was recorded (157 East Reach was, and still is, The Racehorse Inn: there is still a small shop next door though unoccupied at present, and Silver Street is a few paces away).

On his return, Fred went into the bar, and ordered a quart of beer. It was handed to him through a window between the kitchen and the bar along with two glasses. From her position in the passage, Petherick said she saw him pour a glass of beer and then enter the front room with it in his hand. He went to where Annie was sitting and offered her the drink. Petherick did not see what happened next, but it is highly likely that Annie Took the proffered glass. This was about a quarter to eleven at night, and Petherick then moved to stand by the glass door that led out into the street. She watched Ripley leave the front room, and claimed in court to hear him say he would kill the **** before exiting into the street.
In her evidence, Petherick stated she saw something shiny in Ripley's hand, which looked like a knife. She then said to him "I would not if I was you: sit down and be quiet". Such a comment suggests familiarity with Ripley as a regular patron; otherwise, such words could be regarded as impertinent from a servant who was probably in her early twenties. Did Petherick like Ripley, and hope he might take notice of her? There is nothing more vengeful than a thwarted female, and Petherick's evidence to the court does seem to set the scene with prejudice towards Ripley.

Ripley called out to Annie from the street, asking her to come out to join him. Twice he called her, but she only responded the second time. He waited by the glass front door for Annie to join him; the two walked out into the street and the others from the front room also made their way outside – Hodge, Warren and Russell. They apparently stood watching as Fred and Annie walked some distance away, apparently talking.

A different witness – Elizabeth, wife of James Hodge – said the couple conversed under a gas lamp a few yards away for a short time while she stood at the entrance to the Crown & Tower Inn. Hodge had seen Annie and Fred together once before but not recently, and she also saw Annie arrive with Richard Russell that night. She corroborated the offer of drink for Annie but also added that Fred had requested they shake hands with each other, which they did, before he left the premises a second time. She heard Ripley call out to Annie to come outside, and saw them walk to the small bonnet shop in Silver Street some twenty yards away where the pair of them conversed for several minutes. Hodge & Warren crossed the road, possibly to get a better look at what was going on between Ripley and Rowsell, from where they saw Fred raise his hand as if to strike Annie, who then staggered back into the road, screamed, and then moved towards the two female onlookers. Hodge never heard the conversation between the two of them as they were standing face to face when he struck Annie, but she caught up with the victim at the door of the inn. Ripley just walked off along Silver Street.

Annie was saying nothing when Hodge enquired of her what had happened; instead she was holding her neck, and Hodge could see that Annie's throat had been cut. Annie was shuffled into the inn, and medical care sent for. Under questioning by the Judge, it was established that Annie, Hodge and Selina Warren all lived in Penny's Brick-yard and therefore knew each other quite well. Warren in her turn confirmed the evidence already given, and it transpired that Helen Petherick had seen Fred and Annie together regularly up to six weeks before this terrible event. There was even the suggestion that, till recently, Fred and Annie had lived together as husband and wife.

Under cross-examination, Petherick stated that Ripley was in the Militia, and that he kept company with Annie after returning from camp. Service with the militia was similar to that of the Territorials today. She also stated that Annie had "taken up" with Richard Russell only recently, and then made an odd statement that she had no knowledge of Ripley paying for a jacket for Annie. This was probably an omission by the reporter who chose to record an answer to a question or statement that will forever remain a mystery.
Petherick was also keen to impress the court that she had known Annie for some time and was aware of Annie's employment in a collar

factory, of which there were a couple in Taunton at the time. In fact, she stated that Annie washed her collars for her, and also those for Ripley … who she judged to have been sober on the night in question.

The question of the jacket came up again when Hodge was cross-examined. Impressing on the court that she was not in the habit of frequenting public houses and that she was not "boozy" when in the Crown & Tower Inn – a comment that raised laughter in the courtroom – she denied hearing Ripley say to Annie that he was standing there without a farthing to his name because all his money was on her back. This must be a reference to the jacket. Hodge went on to deny he had stated that Annie had finished with him because she had all she wanted from him, or that he demanded the cost of the jacket back, or the jacket itself. She also said she had not heard Annie refuse this demand, nor Fred's threat to cut it from her back. Likewise, she did not see them struggle, nor the slap to Annie's face.

The medical man who attended Annie at the inn decided she was in dire need of more assistance than he could render. He ordered her taken to the Taunton and Somerset Hospital at the bottom of East Reach. Mr Rigden, house surgeon at the said institution, told the court that he assisted Dr Iles when he brought in poor Annie. Together, they did all they could to save her life but the cut was too deep, and she died about half an hour after arrival. The police were informed of events and they went in search of the culprit.

Next into the witness box was Richard Russell but the prosecution decided they had no questions for him. Through examination by the defence, Russell made it known that while he knew Annie, he was adamant that they were not a couple. The newspaper report of his evidence is somewhat short and covers his confirmation of events as given by the earlier witnesses, and that Annie had been stabbed. Whether that was the reporter seeking a different word to use or Russell's ignorance of what had brought about Annie's death is unclear. What is clear is that he had known Annie for quite some time, adding to another suggested theory that he had been a partner of some description with her before she went to live with Fred Ripley, and picking back up with her only recently – though he also informed everyone that he wasn't drinking with Annie any more than he was drinking with anyone else. Wonder what he actually meant by that, or was he trying to make less of their relationship to diffuses any gossip?

The court then heard information from one John Bowerman, a shoemaker who lived in a court just off Silver Street, some twenty to twenty-five feet from the bonnet shop where Annie was attacked. He had seen Ripley and a woman while on his way to the Crown & Tower, and they were in the same place when he returned home. He heard the woman scream when he was about four yards away from them, and saw her injury as she turned in his direction. He watched Ripley walk away from him while the victim made her way as quickly as she could to the inn. Standing where he had seen the couple in conversation, he saw blood on the pavement and on the wall.

Acting Police Sergeant Tom Brown told the court how he found Fred Ripley at the house of Ripley's late brother's widow in Tancred Street and charged him with stabbing Annie Rowsell in Silver Street. He added that Ripley pronounced he had done it. Although he (Brown) warned Ripley to be careful what he said, Ripley went on "I hope I shall be hanged: it was her own fault." It sounded as though Ripley was unaware of the seriousness of her injuries, but the policeman noted that he did not seem excited, though he could see the man had been drinking.

The court rose for lunch, and when they returned, it was time to sum things up. There was no opportunity for the defence to call witnesses to refute the allegations given to support a charge of murder, or perhaps Ripley did not wish to defend his actions. The prosecution summed up for the jury that the facts showed that Ripley was guilty of the crime of wilful murder, motivated by jealousy of her association, or rather her rekindling of an association with Richard Russell with whom Ripley assumed she was intimate. His own statement to the court was then read out by the clerk with a hope that it could explain his actions more clearly.

Fred Ripley wrote that he had been drinking for three or four days up to ten o'clock on 26 December, at which time he went to the Crown & Tower Inn. He sat down in the room with others and saw Annie and Russell, with whom he knew she had been keeping company. He drew her to one side and said "I see you are keeping company with Richard again", to which he claimed she replied "I have a right to". He told her "You left me because I have no more money: it is my money you are wearing on your back". He claimed Annie's reply was "I know it is". Ripley continued "Here I am without a farthing, and only what I've got on. I can see it quite plain. You have got all you wanted out of me, and I'm not wanted." There has to be a moment of pity if this was true; the man was clearly smitten with Annie, and had spent every penny in his pocket to please her. In return, she had discarded him, which she confirmed by saying "I don't want you." That must have hurt – in his heart, his pride, self-esteem and in his pocket. Small wonder that his response was "Pay me back the money you had for the jacket, then you may do as you think proper. I only lent it to you, and didn't give it to you. I shall have the jacket off you." Annie must have started to get enraged at this point because he stated that she then snapped "You won't!". He persisted, saying "I will cut it from you." He then alleged that as he was trying to cut the jacket fastening at the neck, she struck him in the face. In anger and in drink, his response was to bring the knife across her throat, an action for which he was very sorry. They had been together for four years, living as husband and wife despite an age difference between them (she was twelve years his senior) and hoped that the court would be merciful to him.

For the jury, it must have been an awkward situation – or at least it would have been if the case was heard in today's courts. In 1882, the jurors would all have been male, and of a much higher social station than Ripley or Rowsell. The idea of drinking in public houses would have been an anathema to most of them at a time when drunkenness was deemed to be the cause of all the ills the poor ever complained about. Fred and Annie's respective reputations would also have gone against them, and the defence, in summing up, referenced the several days' drinking by the accused. The possibility that Ripley might easily have been suffering *delirium tremens* or shaking caused by too much alcohol was also mentioned.

The Judge told the jury that the prisoner acted on an uncontrollable impulse because of his drinking, adding that he, Ripley, was also a man of low mentality – something that had not come out through any of the evidence given in the case! Maybe he was using that observation because he felt superior to Ripley as he urged the jury to consider that perhaps the accused was not in his right mind. Being mentally subnormal could affect the punishment given at the point of judgement. Maybe the Judge was trying to save Ripley from the death sentence …

Mr Kingslake for the defence continued, clearly hoping for a manslaughter verdict rather than murder, pointing out that the explanation that Ripley was trying to cut the neck fastening of a jacket Annie was wearing that had clearly been bought with Ripley's money was the reason why her throat had been inflicted with such a wound, a wound provoked when she slapped him across the face.

Speaking up for Ripley was the adjutant of the 3rd Somerset Militia, who said Ripley was of good character in his regiment, which was why he had been appointed as waiter in the sergeants' mess. He was followed by Mr Penny, a timber merchant, who had known Fred for ten or twelve years, as he also knew Ripley's father, and that the prisoner always conducted himself well during that time.

Described as a labourer of 21 years of age, Fred Ripley had been noted by reporters to be very nervous and acutely aware of his situation when he entered the dock, and mopped his forehead with a white handkerchief. The court was packed to the gills, some folk queuing for a seat from early that morning. The three-quarters of an hour that the jury took to deliberate must have been excruciating for Ripley and all waiting to hear his fate. Would they see it as murder, or accept it was manslaughter? When they jury resumed their seats, Ripley looked at each one, hoping for some sign of what they had decided. The Foreman was called forward and delivered their verdict of "Wilful Murder" with a recommendation for mercy, and adding that it had been a painful decision for them all. Ripley made no response when asked why the sentence of death should not be pronounced, so the Judge donned the obligatory black cap and ordered him to be hanged by the neck. He saw no cause to be merciful, and extolled Ripley not to expect the sentence to be changed. Sobbing bitterly, Ripley begged for mercy. The Judge said he could not do so, but the jury's recommendation would be sent on (to those in government, who would eventually confirm the sentence and give permission for it to be carried out). As he was led away by two prison warders, Fred turned round and shouted that the servant girl, Petherick had lied. One wonders if anyone gave a single thought to that possibility, either during the case or after the verdict.

So who were these two who held centre stage in Taunton at Christmas 1882, and again in January 1883?

The victim, Annie Rowsell, was buried at Thurlbear, the parish where she had been baptised in March 1844 but her birth was registered in the autumn of the previous year. Her mother, Jane, was unmarried at the time, and the name of the natural father was not recorded. About six weeks after Annie's baptism, her half-brother, Isaac Channing, was baptised in the same church. He was followed by six more children to George Channing and Jane, nee Rowsell. When the 1851 census was taken, Annie was at home with her mother, stepfather and half-siblings at Winterwell Cottage in Thurlbear. By the time the next census was recorded in 1861, Annie was old enough to be working, and was a servant to the Gibson family at 16 The Crescent, Taunton, as a cook. A very responsible post for a girl of only seventeen years old.

By 1871, she is an inmate of the Union Workhouse in Taunton, along with two illegitimate children – a daughter Emma, baptised at Thurlbear in 1864 (and who probably died in 1885), and son Henry. She is described as a farm servant but was unable to undertake farm work whilst an inmate of the workhouse.

It has not been possible to positively identify Annie or her daughter in 1881,but little Henry may have fallen foul of the law by this time. He was noted on Industrial School Ship "Formidable" in Bristol. This was a training ship that was leased from the Admiralty as part of a scheme to deal with the high number of destitute and penniless boys on Bristol's streets. It was financed by several businessmen in the city, and was moored in the Bristol Channel about four hundred yards off Portishead's pier. Initially dealing with those aged between ten and sixteen, many were sent there by the courts where the semi-deliquents were tried on charges of truancy, begging and theft. Not the most salubrious of conditions, it seems to have turned Henry around and by 1891, he had found employment as a groom while lodging in St James Street. Three years later, he was married and soon had a family, from whom there are descendants in the present day.

Piecing together other events in Annie's life, there is a third child somewhere but no clues to its identity or fate have been found, though intense investigations have not been pursued. Annie also went to work in a shirt factory, possibly making collars (the detachable kind that were much favoured by Victorian gentlemen, the ones that were affixed to a shirt by pieces of male jewellery called "collar studs"), where she would have known many of her colleagues as close friends. She certainly seems to have been a popular young lady, and one that caught the eye of the males around her. Among such suitors was one Richard Russell, a labourer whose wife died in 1876. The two of them spent time together, but Annie met Fred Ripley and moved in with him. Annie apparently lived with Fred for quite a while, a period of four years was mentioned, and something happened between them that caused Annie to walk away from their relationship. She must have moved out of wherever they were residing, and – if the evidence given to the court was the truth – chose to do so when Fred ran out of money. The break-up occurred about six weeks before the events detailed in the court case that led to Fred being sentenced to death for her murder. In the short time after parting company with Ripley, Annie had returned to keep company with Richard Russell once again, despite the latter being adamant that they were simply friends.

Fred Ripley was nearly thirteen years younger than Annie, and only 26 years old when he slashed Annie's throat. Perhaps his actions were part of his immaturity, or simply inate jealousy that Annie had moved on … or rather back … to a man more her own age, one she probably had a relationship with before moving in with Fred.

Fred's baptism took place in 1856 in Taunton to William Ripley, a carpenter, and his second wife, Eliza. This was the first child of William's second marriage, and Eliza's first child by her second husband. Born Eliza Brown, she had firstly married cordwainer (shoemaker in so many words) William Jenkins, and in 1852, William Ripley. There were six Ripley children from this marriage – three boys and three girls.

Fred's brother, Henry Ripley, became a printer, married and had four, perhaps five, sons before he died at the early age of twenty-eight. His widow was mentioned during the trial but does not appear to have been called to give evidence. Fred was found in her house in Tancred Street when the police made a return visit to her home, concerning his whereabouts. In 1884, with three young sons to take into consideration, Henry Ripley's widow married again to James Pring – by whom she had another six children before relocating to Bristol. Younger brother, George Ripley became an electrical engineer, and the three sisters seem to have died unmarried. One of them, Caroline Ripley, died at the grand old age of 75 years as a result of a fall in her home in Viney Street. She had lived there for forty years, first as a lodger, then as a boarder, and for the last seventeen years of her life as the sole occupant of the property. Her death was the result of falling out of bed, and she was found when her cousin, Bessie Brown, made one of her frequent visits to check on her. Caroline had fallen once before, sustaining bruised ribs and shoulder but refused to go to hospital or have a nurse come in to care for her. The coroner's verdict in 1936 was death was due to shock following a fall, coupled with pleurisy.

Caroline had been working as a button hole machinist when the 1891 census was taken, and residing as a lodger at 25 Viney Street with Mrs Berry, a widow and retired innkeeper, and her daughter, who happened to be a collar worker. Taunton had a thriving shirt-making industry, so it is nothing extraordinary to find a female in this line of work, but Annie Rowsell was also a collar maker. In 1901, Caroline was still in Viney Street with the same mother and daughter, and she was now a collar maker too. Was she working in the same factory as Annie Rowsell in the late 1870s, when her brother gets entangled emotionally and physically with Annie? By 1911, it is just Caroline boarding with Mrs Berry's daughter in Viney Street, but she has progressed to be a "button-hole forewoman in collar making".

In court, the Judge seemed to suggest that Fred Ripley was "of less than average intelligence". He certainly does not appear to have followed a trade that required any skill or training, but one of his referees told the court that he was well thought of and had been appointed as a waiter in the sergeants' mess. This does appear to be another unskilled role, though the regimen of doing everything by the book would have suited Fred if he was someone who found learning difficult. Certainly in 1871, Fred has no specific employment, and was living at home with several siblings and his widowed mother at 20 Tancred Street.

Nothing has come to the fore concerning Fred's appearance, or character. He certainly seems to have become a broken man through knowing and living with Annie Rowsell, and no-one will ever know what went through his mind on Boxing Night 1882. He claimed he was trying to cut the fastenings on Annie's jacket, a jacket he seems to have paid for, which left him with no money of his own. If Annie suddenly moved her head, she might have caused the injuries herself, rather than Fred viciously and callously slashing her throat. He seems to have casually strolled away after the event, leaving Annie to flee back to the Crown & Tower Inn seeking help for her situation. It might lend itself to the thought that he had no idea how seriously injured Annie was … unless he was totally cold-blooded in his actions. That's where you, the reader, can decide: was her demise his intention when he asked her to join him outside, or was it nothing more than an accident that her throat impacted on his knife? That would be the difference between murder (a pre-meditated act) and manslaughter (death as a result of circumstance).

It has not been possible to identify Fred Ripley on the 1881 census, possibly because he was then serving with, or in the employ of the Somerset Militia, which may have been away from Taunton. In early 1882, using the alias of Samuel Ripley, he spent fourteen days in prison for being drunk with riotous behaviour.

After his arrest, he was held in Taunton Gaol before being charged in Taunton Police Court with the murder of Annie Rowsell. He was then taken to Shire Hall to be tried at 11a.m. in the morning but was remanded to allow the charge to be fully prepared. On 1 February 1883, the verdict "Guilty" was delivered, and the death sentence rendered. It was common practice for the condemned to be allowed to live for a further three Sundays, and during that period, Ripley's sentence was commuted to life imprisonment.

Now, from prison records, it is possible to ascertain that he was five foot seven and three-eights inches in height with a fresh complexion, light brown hair and grey eyes. He had five moles on his back and one on the front of his right ear. He also sported a blue mark on his right forearm and two blue spots were on the back of his right hand. For some reason they also added that he had a hairy chest; to mention this attribute, Fred must have been fairly hirsute!

He served time in a number of different penal institutions including Pentonville, Parkhurst and Portland. In 1897, a letter was sent to the Mayor of Taunton from the Home Office, informing him that Fred Ripley was to be released from gaol because of his health. On 19 July of that year, Fred was a free man and went to live in Bristol as a labourer. On the 1901 census record, he is listed as a patient in the Guinea Street Hospital in Bristol as a bachelor employed as a porter … perhaps at the hospital itself. Ten years on, and he is still unmarried but is now an inmate of the Bristol City Workhouse in Eastville,

Bristol.

In early 1921, Fred Ripley died in the Bristol area at 69 years old.

Richard Russell, the male friend of Annie Rowsell on the night she died, died in 1887, aged 55 years. He was living as a widower at Holway, Taunton, in 1881 with his son David. In 1871, the family – Richard, his wife, and two children – were recorded at Middle Lambrook, Kingsbury Episcopi.

The Crown & Tower Inn was run by Richard Laurence in 1881, along with his wife, Catherine. After his death … also in 1887 … at 43 years old, Catherine became the innkeeper. At the end of March 1890, she found herself in court again, this time for selling brandy which was 30.4° under proof, for which she pleaded guilty, and was fined ten shillings plus costs by magistrates. In 1895, she married widower Thomas Branchflower, carpenter, who lived round the corner in Alma Street, and she was still at the Crown & Tower in 1901, though without her second husband. Catherine's death took place in 1924. She was 78 years of age, and living in Mansfield Road as a widow. Her estate was placed into the hands of a solicitor and accountant, George Curry, who was possibly her nearest living relative (her maiden name was Curry when she married Richard Lawrence in 1865).

Helen Petherick is not given in the newspaper reports with an age, or even a hint of an age. The only entry of this name on the 1881 census was found as a cook in London. Aged 22, she was a servant to the Belflage family and gave her place of birth as Buck in Cornwall. An entry for a Helena Petherick, 22 years old, occurs at Hatherleigh in Devon, where she was born. This Helena was a domestic servant living at home, and still at home in 1891. It would not preclude her from a spell of service in Taunton between 1881 and 1891, and Petherick is not a local name. A third possibility is Helena E Pederick, another servant residing in North Burcombe in Wiltshire in 1881. She was also born in Devon and acting as a lady's maid to the Rev and Mrs Savage. The Cornish born candidate seems the most probable, but nothing more is known about her beyond the evidence she gave to the court in 1883.

Elizabeth Hodge, wife of James Hodge, labourer, were living near the Dolphin Inn in 1891 with three children. They must have needed larger accommodation than that occupied at 36 South Street in 1881.

Finally, Selina Warren, widow of Taunton, who was the last of the named individuals to give evidence against Fred Ripley. In 1881, she was working as a laundress at 13 Cottage Row, with her four children and a boarder. She was then only 34 years of age, and hailed from Bishops Hull. Her husband Thomas had died in 1879 at 31 years, when they had been married for about eleven years. Nee Corner, Selina went on to marry again in 1886, and her death was registered in late 1915 as Selina Bryer, aged 69.

Did any of those who featured in the case of Fred Ripley and Annie Rowsell ever reveal their part in this drama to their families? No mention was made of Caroline's connection to Fred at the inquest into her death, or in the newspapers reporting the same. Was it common knowledge in Henry Rowsell's descendants that his mother died in such a horrific fashion at the hands of Fred Ripley? Did Fred's immediate family ever talk in hushed tones about the years he spent in prison, or why he never married or had children? In most families, there are secrets and scandal; who knows if it is the same for those in and around Taunton today bearing the surname of Ripley or Rowsell?

8. THE PRINGS

The name of Pring featured in the Fred Ripley case of 1882.
Fred's brother married a lady named Jessie Staples and, after she was
widowed in 1881 with young children to care for, she married for a
second time to James Pring in 1884 at Taunton St James parish church.

By 1891, James Pring had relocated his family- including his four
Ripley step-children - to reside at 41 Corbett Street, Bristol, where he
was employed as a corn porter. This census record places his birth to
about 1855 in Taunton, and he died in 1918 in Bristol district.
In 1881, James was unmarried and living at home in Half Moon Court
(North Street), Taunton, with his widowed mother Maria. By searching
several census returns, it was possible to locate a number of older
siblings, some of whom were recorded on the 1841 census with James
and Maria Pring in Turkey Court, Wilton.
This older James Pring was a cabinet maker journeyman in 1841; that
is to say someone who had completed his apprenticeship to a trade but
was still proving his ability in the craft to be abe to take apprentices of
his own. He may have been in court in 1843 for not paying a road toll,
for which he was acquitted. The most likely death for him is registered
in 1846 … some nine years before the younger James was born!
Across the census records, Maria is shown as a widow by 1851, which
puts that death into its place in this family but by 1861, Maria has a
son and a daughter born after her husband's demise – Eliza in 1853
and the said James the younger the following year. Were those two
children illegitimate, or did Maria raise two children born to one of her
daughters as her own?

Another Pring fell foul of the law in 1885.
On 30 December in Taunton Police Court, George Adams, a mason of
King Street, Thomas Edward Pring, labourer of Mount Lane, and
Thomas' wife, Sarah Pring, were charged with the theft of fourteen
paraffin lamps, nine benzoline lamps, two dozen tops of lamps, three
dozen burners, two galvanized tubs and one lamp bracket. It was
Christmas Eve, and Acting-Sergeant Brown was in Mount Street at the
rear of John Godden's premises – which John Godden owned the
items robbed. The said goods were taken from his East Street property

whilst the building was on fire (the reason Brown was there in the first place) – and the eagle-eyed policeman noticed Sarah lurking about. When she saw him, she moved off and immediately after her rapid exit, Adams' head popped up over Godden's garden wall before the man jumped over it, into the lane where Brown was on duty. Brown told Adams he would be charged with being on the premises for illegal purposes, and the reply was "You know I have been helping at the fire". Brown then visited the Adams' and the Prings' houses where he found the stolen articles as previously listed. John Godden identified them all as his own property. Perhaps Adams had been helping with the fire … and helping himself in the process!

Adams was sentenced to two months' imprisonment for participating in the robbery while Godden's livelihood was burning. Thomas Pring received one month's imprisonment, presumably for receiving the stolen goods or transporting the booty from the scene of the robbery … err … fire, while his wife had her sentence of one month remitted because she was needed by her eight children. Yes, eight children … and that was an average family for the period.

This is where things got more interesting when it was discovered that Sarah Pring was George Adams' daughter. The robbery was very much a family affair, but who was the "brains" behind it, and did they also start the fire to gain access to the goods?

The two families united in 1864 when Thomas and Sarah were married. By 1891, the couple were residing at 1 Starplatt (near Mount Lane), occupying three main rooms with their five children. Four more children were found with them in 1881. Both records show Thomas Pring as working as a mason's labourer, a trade he was in while living at home in 1861 in Paul Street with parents James and Joan Pring. James and Joan? Any connection to the James mentioned earlier? Certainly this family group has a connection to Wilton, as did the earlier Prings but … as yet … no common ancestor has been located. The Adams family was also Taunton based but has yet to be fully extended. Who knows what other offences might be uncovered?

The name of Pring also featured in a hearing in the Taunton Coroner's Court in August 1885. From the *West Somerset Free Press, etc: 22 Aug 1885 edition*, the following information was noted:

On Tuesday morning, the dead body of William Pring (59), an Army pensioner, was found hanging by a rope from the bannister at the top of the stairs in his home, in Pig Market. He had lost his wife about six weeks earlier, and since then, he was said to have been very strange in his manner and, at times, despondent. A neighbour noticed the key in the lock on the outside of his door on the Tuesday morning about half past nine, and on going upstairs to find him, she discovered him hanging from the bannister.

Information was given to the police, and Sergeant Broadribb cut the body down. He found two small boxes on the floor, and the deceased had evidently used them for the purpose of standing on until he managed to affix the rope around his neck. He then kicked them away.

The body is supposed to have been hanging there for about nine hours before it was found. One wonders how his family coped with his death under such circumstances.

His late wife, Eliza, came from Milverton, Somerset, and they were together at 6 Batts Court in 1881. William was working as a labourer, in keeping with about 75% of the male population at that time, but the 1871 census indicates he was a pensioner. This would not be an old age pensioner as we have today (the state pension in the UK was first paid in in 1909 for those aged 70 and above) and is more likely to be a pension paid to those who had fulfilled military service.

A Private William Pring was pensioned out of the 14th Regiment of Foot in 1857, two years after the regiment had served in the Crimea. He received 6d (probably per week), but this was only a temporary award. His pension expired in 1859. This might be the same William Pring as the suicide, or he could be the Pte William Pring who saw service in Cawnpore, India in 1851 as part of the 70th (Surrey) Regiment of Foot, or even the man of the same name who was in Athlone in Ireland while the previous candidate was out in the heat of India. In Ireland, Pte William Pring was with the 14th (Buckinghamshire) Regiment of Foot. Despite the place of birth or residence of a soldier, they could serve in any regiment, as recruiting bands often set up their stall in market towns to encourage young men to take the Queen's shilling. Sometimes, a soldier would transfer between regiments for a variety of reasons, making these four individuals candidates for the poor soul who found life so unbearable he resorted to suicide.

The couple were again in Batts Court off Fore Street, and William said he was born in Wilton. At this time (1871), there was a single child living at home – a son named Francis who was born about 1856 in the British East Indies, who was employed as a silk factory boy on that record. This exotic place of birth … probably a reference to India … explains the absence of William Pring from the 1861 census and places the suggested Private 2011 William Pring of the 70th Regiment of Foot as someone worth more detailed investigation because he was in India in the first three months of 1851.

Ten years later, Pte 2011 Pring was still with the same regiment but at sea on census night, between India and New Zealand. It also appears that this William Pring of the 70th regiment had two children in Cawnpore (Sarah 1851-1852 & Elizabeth 1853) and possible another Sarah in 1861. In 1851 and 1853, his wife is named as Bridget. There might be two more children born in India – Francis in 1855 and Jane three years later – and even another son, John, in 1862 in New Zealand. Certificates have not been accessed to confirm or refute any connection to Private 2011, or to Taunton.

In 1848, William Pring (son of James Pring) was married to a Bridget McNurtey in Ireland. On 2 June 1868, widower William Pring, a private in the army and son of James Pring, married at Taunton Holy Trinity church to Elizabeth Downing, widow (daughter of Samuel Reed), thus adding a greater probability of the India/New Zealand connection belonging to the suicide in 1885.

The quoted place of birth as Wilton on the 1871 census certainly puts William as possibly related to Thomas Edward Pring the thief of 1885. William claims to have been born about 1825, which lines him up with a William Pring baptised that year in Wilton to James & Mary (Shute) Pring. Not only does it further connect the suicide with the Irish marriage in 1848, the children in India and New Zealand, followed by a second marriage in Taunton, it also makes him the uncle of miscreant Thomas Edward Pring, whose encounter with the law took place some four months after William's sad end. Was this the last straw for poor old William, his nephew sinking to petty theft? If only he was here now, he could not only confirm what is suggested in this chapter, he could regale us with tales of military life in the Crimea, in India, Ireland and New Zealand.

9. THOMAS HANCOCK

One more, one more. This collection warrants one more story, one more tale, one more crime. So, here is the tale of Thomas Hancock who, in 1876, was charged with attempting to murder his wife. Immediately, it was of sufficient interest to be considered further, and hence its inclusion was secured.

On 21 October 1876, Thomas attempted to kill his wife, Esther Hancock. Details printed in the *Chard & Ilminster News* (11 Nov 1876 edtn) helped to reveal what had taken place when the matter came to trial in the magistrates court, and this was expanded by a further article in the *Bridgewater Mercury* (8 Nov 1876 edtn).
Thomas was aged 40 years when he tried to kill his wife. The couple had been separated for about two months, following him being bound over to keep the peace towards her. This order came into force in May, and ran for a six month period, but Thomas had been unable to find sufficient sureties and therefore found himself in gaol until he did. Released at the end of June 1876, he went back to living with Esther and their children but they separated again in late September or early October after two months together.

On the night in question, Thomas, a painter, met his wife in East Reach, just opposite Chorley's baker's shop (1871 census lists an Eli Chorley as a baker at 143 East Reach). Mrs Hancock had a young child in her arms, and Thomas took it from her, kissed it and took the child across the road to the baker's establishment. The child's age is never given, and it is likely to have been their second daughter, Eliza Jane, who would have been about one to one and a half at the time. Purchasing a slice of cake for the girl, he returned the child to his wife and asked her to go with him to Alma Street. He reasoned that he had a lot of money to give and, since Esther told the court he had given her nothing more than half a crown since leaving her, she went along with the suggestion, taking the lttle girl with them.
In Alma Street, they met their eldest boy, who had been sent to fetch tea and sugar from his grandmother who lived near there. Thomas told the boy to return to his grandmother and wait in her house until he came for him. The boy, Thomas Jnr, was nine years of age. This might

seem a young age to be out and about on the streets of Taunton at night, but the town was completely different in 1876 – less inhabitants, no motorised traffic, even the streets were fewer than today.

Thomas and Esther continued walking, and together they visited a labourer named John Wood at his cottage in East Reach. Wood had taken in their young son, identified only as "Alby", when Thomas had been placed in gaol for failure of finding securities.

In court, Wood said he had not received anything for taking in the child, and did so out of the goodness of his heart. Alby – or Albert John Hancock to give his full name, though he was known as Alby all his life – was six years old when he moved in with Wood and his wife. While they were there talking with John Wood, and Thomas had hoped his son (Alby) would still be awake despite their visit being after eight o'clock in the evening, Thomas kept kissing his daughter, and had his arm round his wife's shoulder.

Esther claimed that whilst they were in Wood's cottage, her husband whispered to her that one of them would be in the cemetery before long, and that he was asking to come back with her to her home. She was then lodging with two of her four children in one room, and she told him that he would not be allowed to join them. On hearing this, Thomas was not a happy man, He started to curse and swear, banging his fists on the table and saying how much he loved his children. Esther begged him to be quiet, aware that Mrs Wood had returned and was within earshot (even though Mrs Wood was never called to give evidence in court) but he would not … or could not? Perhaps his emotions had got the better of him at this point, and he could not control himself after she refused to take him back.

As soon as the chance arose, Esther slipped out of Wood's house and started to make her way back to her meagre lodgings. She was still carrying her daughter in her arms, but heard Thomas coming up behind her. His stalking of his wife led to her starting to run as she reached the top of the court on East Reach. She was heading towards the hospital to get to Union Place (presumably where she was residing) but the burden of the child made swift flight impossible. Thomas caught up with her, grabbed her by the hair and pulled her head back. Feeling something across her throat, she put her right hand up to her face, sustaining an injury to her hand in the process. Thomas ran off, and Esther realised she was bleeding. She screamed out "Murder!" and a crowd gathered around her just as she started to faint. Her child was

lifted from her by somebody, and another person caught her as she fell. She was taken to the Taunton and Somerset Hospital for treatment, where the medical officer on duty found her throat had been cut but not severely. In fact, the wound on her hand was more serious.
About five minutes after she arrived seeking medical assistance, her husband was brought in with his throat slashed. He had attempted suicide and managed to sever his jugular vein, putting him in a more serious condition than his victim. Thomas was out cold on arrival but the skill of the doctor on duty saved his life, though he took longer to recover than Esther. For some hours, he was in a critical condition, his life in the balance.

Thomas George Coombs Hancock was born in Wiveliscombe, Somerset and was living with his parents, George and Eliza, in Silver Street, Taunton (next to Govier's Court) by 1861. By 1871, he was living with wife Esther and their two boys in Moores Court, (just after No 32) Silver Street, and working as a journeyman painter. By 1881, Esther was living on her own in Great Court as a married woman with five children – sons Thomas (1875), Albert (1870) and Frederick William (1877) and daughters Alice Mary Eames (1873) and Eliza Jane (1875).
Clearly, whatever the outcome of the attempted murder case in 1876, they had been friendly enough for her to conceive Frederick in late 1876. She may have been expecting this child when the incident occurred, and probably when she gave her account of the matter in court. Perhaps the child wasn't her husband's … but no, let's not entertain that idea.

In the magistrates' court, witness John Wood mentioned that Thomas had drunk a pint of cider with him before following his wife, Esther Hancock, out of the cottage. Thomas returned to Wood's home about five minutes later, blood flowing from his neck and utterly speechless. The police subsequently found a partly-open razor with wet blood still adhering to it in a garden adjacent to Wood's place; Esther later identified it as belonging to her husband. Wood must have been instrumental in getting the injured man to hospital, thus saving his life, and thereby causing the legal case to begin.
The law saw suicide as a crime and, initially, it would have been an investigation into him attempting to take his own life that would be required, but in reality, the police failed to charge him with that

offence. Instead, they opted to prosecute him for attempted murder.

When Hancock, who was without defence counsel, was asked if he had any questions he would like to put to the witness (Wood), Thomas said "No", adding that he did not remember being at Wood's house on the night in question. Could this be amnesia, the result of too much drink, or simply a ploy to excuse his behaviour of that night?
In his own defence, Thomas told the court that his wife had been unfaithful to him and he had suspected her fidelity for some years. Calling Esther a "bad woman", he said that she was always wanting him to take work away from Taunton. About six or seven years previous, around the time of Albert John's birth, Thomas came home from work early, about half-past three in the afternoon, and found Esther drunk but in the company of two Marines. Thomas was then lodging with a Mr Chick, suggesting the couple were separated at that time. Some eighteen months to two years after that incident, Thomas was working for a Mr Blake at Martock and wrote to his wife that he would be returning home on the five o'clock train. Instead, he sneakily came back at 9.15 (not given whether in morning or evening) and found he could not get into the house. Soon after trying to gain entry, he said he spotted a man running from the property. He also related that he had once worked in Bridgewater and returned to find some of his furniture had been removed; his wife being the only person who could have taken them from his home.
The magistrates clearly felt there was definitely a case to answer, and despite Thomas claiming she was a bad wife, they sent the case to be heard at the county assizes to be held at Exeter. Hancock was held in custody until that time.

It was only a couple of weeks later that the case came before a judge at the Winter Assizes for Somerset, held in Exeter Castle.
Thomas' age is now recorded as only 38, and the same evidence as already given was repeated, and reported in slightly greater detail by the newspapers (the two accounts have been combined for the purpose of painting the picture here). Clearly, Thomas had tried to kill his wife for whatever motive, and the Jury found him Guilty. His sentence was reported a week later, and he was to serve ten years' penal servitude.

Now his absence from the 1881 census is explained! Thomas was halfway through his prison sentence, but it is unclear in how many prisons he spent his term. In January 1877, he was removed from the Taunton County Gaol to Pentonville with a release date of August 1884. Must have got time off for good behavior.

By 1891, he was back in Taunton, and working as a painter once more. He was also the father of twin daughters, and living in Paynes Court, (just before No 156) East Reach … with his wife, Esther. At least, the twins were possibly his. Their date of birth is quoted as 30 Jul 1885 on later records which, if he served the designated full term of ten years, with release in 1886, precludes him from being their father.
Thomas and Esther are recorded together on the 1901 and 1911 census records. He died in 1913, and Esther six years later (as Hester).

In 1911, Thomas gives his trade as a house painter, adding "unable to follow work", and he has a grand-daughter, Olive Hancock (born about 1900, Taunton) under his roof. Olive was the youngest daughter of his eldest son and namesake. She has descendants born in Taunton in the 1990s surnamed Janaway and Perry, each one able to claim descent from a man who served time in prison for trying to kill his wife but who came back to her and lived with her for the next 27 years.
The Hancock family can be traced back through the generations at Wiveliscombe and at Milverton to a John Hancock who lived through the English Civil War of the 17th century.
It is amazing what you find in families!

IN THE NEWS

Taunton Courier & Western Advertiser: 8 April 1840 edtn:

Calendar of Prisoners to be tried at Somerset Lent Assizes at Taunton on April 2nd, 1840 ... including;

Ann Woodburn - wilful murder of her bastard child – Not Guilty
Samuel Hears – stealing 2 umbrellas at Staplegrove – 3 months prison
Mary Baxter – stealing 20 lbs of lead – Not Guilty of receiving
Henry Haynes – stealing cheese – 1 month in House of Correction
Eliza Rowchest – stealing an apron – 6 months prison
John Palfrey & William Palfrey – stealing two ducks
       John received 3 months in prison; William – Not Guilty
Ann Collins – stealing a great coat – 2 months prison
William Spurdle – bigamy – No prosecution
Sarah Payne – stealing turnips – 4 months prison
John & Nancy Rawlins – stealing peas - both Not Guilty
John Sandy – stealing a coat and 2 pairs of gloves - Acquitted

Taunton Courier & Western Advertiser: 17 July 1872 edtn:

Taunton Police Court – A little boy named Alfred Hembrow was charged with stealing a pair of boots of John Redwood of Oake Mills. Hembrow went to the mill begging and after he left, the boots were missed. They were subsequently found where he was.
Sentenced to fourteen days in prison and nine strokes of the birch rod.

Hembrow obviously did not learn his lesson. He was back in court in 1882, aged about 20, for robbery. He and his victim were discharged naval artillerymen, and were visiting Hembrow's mother at Norton Fitzwarren.

10. THERE HAS TO BE A HIGHWAYMAN

During the 18th century, it was a common occurrence for travellers to be waylaid by desperate men riding horses, usually black, and wielding guns who demanded "Your money or your life!". They were known as highwaymen if mounted, while those unfortunate enough not to afford, own or steal a horse but following the same line of work … if you can call it that … were deemed to be footpads. Both types were prevalent in every county in England, including Somerset, but nothing has revealed itself for such an individual in and around Taunton. There has to be a highwayman in this volume, and the best I could find is full of wonderful information and intrigue.

The actual hold-up took place near Congresbury in what is now North Somerset but the miscreant was tried in Taunton, thus furnishing the necessary link needed for inclusion here.

The year was 1831, and it became the last robbery on horseback to take place in the county.

The perpetrator was Richard Hewlett, a married man with three children, who had been a farmer near Huish, Somerset. His farm adjoined that of one Charles Capell Hardwick, who joins this tale as the victim. Hardwick was also a farmer in Huish and on the night in question, he was returning from a successful day at Bristol market, with plenty of cash in his pockets. Not all of it was his own, as he often acted as an agent for others. As he made his way home to Huish, he found himself riding alongside his old neighbour, Hewlett, and they fell into genial conversation. About a mile and a half from Congresbury, Hewlett suddenly produced a pistol and shot his companion in the shoulder. He presumably helped himself to some or all of the money in Hardwick's pockets before riding off at great speed. … or perhaps he just rode off, preferring freedom to loot. The chase was on!

Despite being shot, Charles Hardwick rode after his assailant and caught up with him at the bridge leading to Congresbury Moor, only half a mile from where the shooting had occurred. Hewlett struck him again, this time using a bludgeon on the head before galloping away in the direction of Congresbury village. Picking himself up, Hardwick managed to follow his assailant again, and succeeded in catching him when the ruffian's horse fell while trying to avoid an oncoming cart. The two men tussled and struggled on the ground, and Hardwick was struck more blows to the head by Hewlett. Whilst admiring his fortitude, one has to wonder how thick-skulled Hardwick was to receive a number of blows after receiving a shoulder wound and still remain conscious enough to give chase. Hewlett must also have been questioning how to get out of this situation, and he opted to produce a seven inch long dagger from about his person, stabbing Hardwick in the side. Rather than falling to the floor, Hardwick clung like a limpet to the highwayman and called out for aid and assistance, which eventually arrived.

On April Fool's Day 1831, or Good Friday if you prefer, the Somerset Assizes began, sitting in Taunton Castle, in the same courtroom that had heard Judge Jeffrey pronounce the fate of those who had supported Monmouth's Rebellion. Hewlett's trial took place at the Saturday sessions and he faced 12 charges. There was a huge clamour to be there in the courtroom to watch and hear the proceedings. The under-sheriff with his javelin-men and other court officers found themselves struggling to keep what was described as "a promiscuous crowd" under control as spectators scrambled to occupy that area of the courtroom reserved for those of the legal profession. By the time the Judge entered and took his place, there wasn't a single seat vacant, with some having to stand through the proceedings.
Hewlett was brought into court along with several other prisoners and all were placed in the dock. He was dressed in a blue coat that was partly buttoned, and drab trousers. He held a pencil and paper and took great interest in every one of the jury as they were sworn in. The other prisoners were then removed from the courtroom, leaving Hewlett as the first case to be heard. When the charges were read out to him, he firmly stated he was "Not Guilty".

The first witness was Charles Capell Hardwick, the man Hewlett had robbed and attempted to murder – several times. Before he could be sworn in to give evidence, there was an objection. This required legal discussion before the case could proceed. Described as "a gentlemanly-looking young man" Hardwick described himself as a grazier living at Huish, and also an agent for wool that required him to possess large amounts of money. He described the events of October 21st in the previous year, how he left Bristol about six in the evening and, with about £30 in his pocket (or the equivalent of earning just under £26,500 in 2020), he overtook Hewlett at a place called Newland's Batch some five miles from the city and about seven from Congresbury. Claiming to be a stranger, Hewlett asked if he could keep company with Hardwick, at least until they reached Congresbury. They rode together until they reached Rhodyate Hill, where they dismounted and walked down the hill, probably to give their mounts a slight respite in the journey. This was about half a mile from an inn in Congresbury and at this point, a copy of a map was presented to the Judge to better show the area while Hewlett slipped a note to the counsel for his defence. Hardwick continued, revealing how they rode together through Congresbury, and over a bridge to a place called the Heath. He stated there used to be a gate there but it had been removed, and that it was about a mile and a half from the inn. Between Congresbury and the Heath, the pair, who had not always ridden side by side, met a cart. Hewlett was on the left side of the road, rather than behind Hardwick, a position he had favoured along the road from Congresbury. Hardwick then heard the retort of a pistol being fired and his horse was frightened. He felt a jolt in his shoulder and thought he glimpsed a bright flash but clearly had no idea he had been shot. He managed to pull up his horse and gave hot pursuit to his travelling companion who was galloping back towards Congresbury. Hardwick said he passed a cart, the same one they had overtaken when riding in the opposite direction before the pistol shot. Coming level with Hewlett, Hardwick reached out for the bridle of his assailant's horse, receiving several blows on the head for his efforts. Hewlett never spoke, and Hardwick fell to the ground under the rain of blows from a cudgel or stick. He got to his feet, remounted, and continued to give continued chase as Hewlett was still in his sight. As he got closer, Hewlett was saying something - which Hardwick thought was probably several threats but he could not hear the words clearly. Hewlett continued to ride, going through the village at speed, then over the bridge, with Hardwick still tight on his tail and calling out to all he passed to stop the rider in front.

Reaching what was known as the Kent road, another cart came into view and Hewlett's horse fell trying to swerve around it, as did Hardwick's mount. Getting onto his feet with surprising agility, Hardwick leapt on Hewlett and they scuffled and fought, rolling on the ground, during which struggle Hardwick was stabbed several times.

Hewlett was holding something in one hand, and used it to beat Hardwick about the head. Hewlett jumped onto his horse, intending to ride off like the wind but Hardwick grabbed hold of the beast's bridle and clung on. The pistol had been dropped at some point, and Hardwick shifted his grip to holding Hewlett's coat. Now someone came and helped Hardwick. Together, they hustled the highwayman into the inn at Congresbury, where three others helped to restrain Hewlett from further flight.

During his evidence, the Judge had noticed that Hardwick was holding his hand and arm in a certain position and enquired as to the reason for this. Hardwick stated he had lost full use of his left limb, but could still do some things with it but was fairly limited. He remembered that he had seen Hewlett at Bristol market several times in the past, and he was therefore aware not only of Hardwick's business but of the amounts of cash he was likely to possess. Isn't most probable that Hewlett recognised his one-time neighbour, recalled his type of employment and decided to consider a money transfer – from Hardwick's pockets into his own?

Next came the cart driver they had encountered at the Heath. Making his way from Weston-Super-Mare to Bath market with a cartload of fish and fowl, John Hill rendered his version of what he had seen. He had heard something but did not place it as a pistol shot because of the rumbling from his cart's wheels. A short time later, the two men that had been travelling in the opposite direction to his cart rode past him, and then he encountered them for a third time after Hardwick had detained Hewlett at the bridge, declaring to Hill that he, Hardwick, had been shot by his prisoner.

Others were called to relate the various details of what they saw and heard concerning the two men, including the constable who took possession of Hewlett thereafter. He examined the contents of Hewlett's pockets, finding a razor in his waistcoat pocket, a tin of gunpowder, sixteen bullets, a map of England and Wales, two flints for guns or pistols and a list of fairs among other papers. Pistols were retrieved from the water near the bridge, one of which was loaded, and each contained flints that were similar to those in Hewlett's possession, as was the case with the bullet. That might have been argued as circumstantial in a modern-day situation, but in the 1830s, it was virtually a slam-dunk.

The pistols had been fixed together to form a sort of double-barrelled weapon, and then there was a stick. Sticks were often carried as the mark of a gentleman rather than for ambulatory purposes but this one was about thirty inches long with a dagger top and weighted with lead. It certainly sounds like a weapon disguised to look like a gentleman's accoutrement. It also explains how Hewlett was able to stab his victim and almost immediately hit him about the head with something heavy. Hardwick's light-coloured coat was shown to the court with a dark black mark on the left shoulder, and a hole where a missile from the pistol had penetrated the cloth. At the time of the trial, the pistol ball was still embedded in Hardwick's shoulder, and being stabbed had resulted in breathing difficulties as air was collecting under Hardwick's skin. He had received sixteen days of treatment from a medical man who was quite expecting him not to survive his injuries.

It was then the turn of Richard Hewlett to refute the allegations made by the prosecution. In a fairly loud voice so that all in the court could hear, he said "I've got to say, my Lord, that I am innocent of this charge. I never intended to do Mr Hardwick any harm, nor do I think I did him any."
He paused.
"I think, my Lord, nothing I can now say will avail me."
He declined to say anything further, and everything now hinged on the findings of the Jury.

It is hardly surprising that the Jury returned a verdict of Guilty after only a few minutes' deliberation. After the Clerk of the Court asked Hewlett of any previous convictions against him,and receiving a negative response, the Judge donned the obligatory black cap and solemnly delivered the sentence of death upon him.
Throughout the trial, Hewlett kept a straight and expressionless face, giving away nothing concerning his feelings. He did pass a number of notes to his counsel and also made notes while the Judge advised the Jury of their responsibilities. Placed in irons, he turned to leave the dock after sentencing, and remarked to those nearest to him that it would be useless to consider a petition to save him.
It later transpired that Hewlett had been convicted of horse stealing some five years earlier and, with the promise of a relative giving him £20 providing he left for America, he spent no time in gaol.
Reappearing after a decent interval, he went back to his family and

never left these shores.

He was described as strong and muscular, fairly tall at five-nine or five-ten in height, with sandy-coloured hair and whiskers. One of the witnesses described him as having dark hair at the time of the incident, and being clean-shaven, so it is likely that he had dyed his hair as a slight disguise in 1831, whereas his natural colour came through by the time of his trial and he had opted to grow whiskers, perhaps to give him an air of respectability and authority.

A final comment in the article reporting these proceedings stated that the cart that caused Hewlett's horse to fall, which subsequently brought down Hardwick's horse, contained Hardwick's brother and sister, who failed to recognise their sibling during the scuffle that ensued close by them. In fact, they took no notice of the event at all, and simply continued on their way.

Richard Hewlett was confined in Ilchester Gaol and hanged there on the prescribed day of execution. He was buried in Ilchester on 22nd April 1831, aged 37, as a resident of the prison itself. He was baptised in 1793 at Wick St Lawrence, son of Samuel and Pheby Hewlett, and married by licence at Winscombe in 1812 to Joanna Brawdy. Two daughters have been found for this couple – Emma who was born in 1813, baptised in 1816 and buried in 1818, and Matilda who was baptised at the same time as her sister. The third child referred to in the newspaper report has yet to be identified.

By 1841, Joanna Hewlett was living in Bedminster, near Bristol, with the James family and described herself as "Independent". She probably had little choice but make her own way in the world. It would not further her chances if they knew she was the widow of an executed highwayman. Her fate remains a mystery after 1841 but her first name, like the surname of Hewlett, could be subjected to a number of variants. Perhaps she left England, especially as Bristol was a main port for emigrants to America.

Her daughter, Matilda, is equally as mysterious, though a woman of that same name appears in a Calendar of Prisoners for the Somerset Sessions held at Wells in March 1849, alongside one Hannah Lyde, for breaking into a dwelling-house of a Lazarus Holbrook and stealing two gowns and other articles.

The courage and perseverance of Hardwick to capture Hewlett became quite a talking point but it seems likely that his injury meant he was never the same again. He was baptised in 1799 at Kewstoke, son of Thomas and Sarah Hardwick; never married; and was buried in early July 1849 at 50 years of age. His father dealt with Charles' estate.

Whilst Hardwick's burial took place at Hutton, near Weston-Super Mare (as are many of the places connected with this particular case), there is a fine granite memorial to him at Congresbury, complete with a valedictory verse:

"He was of such courage
that being attacked
by a Highwayman
on the Heath in this parish
October 21st 1830
and fearfully wounded by him
He pursued his assailant
and having overtaken him
in the centre of this village
delivered him to Justice"

Two reports of his passing are worthy of inclusion here – one because of the glowing words used to impress the reader, and the other for opting to remind the public of his heroic actions:

Sherborne Mercury (14 July 1849 edtn) - Deaths:
Charles Capell Hardwick, age 50 – "His decease is severely felt by numerous and attached family, and deeply regretted by a large circle of friends. Few have acquired more extensive and deserved respect for high integrity of principle in the various transactions of life or acquired more sincere regard from all classes of society"

Bath Chronicle & Weekly Gazette (12 Jul 1849 edtn):
"Death of Charles Capell Hardwick of Huish, Congresbury, a gentleman who enjoyed the confidence and commanded respect of as large a circle of friends as any resident in the North Marsh. His name will recall in mind of many a recollection of the murderous attack made upon him some twenty years since. On the occasion referred to Mr Hardwick was returning from Bristol market, etc., etc."

Whilst highwaymen have achieved a legendary position in history alongside smugglers and pirates, even those who were of the blackest of characters, their romanticism doesn't always live on, and in the case of Richard Hewlett – who may not have been a highwayman in the real sense of the name, but rather someone who took an opportunity to get his hands on some easy money whilst travelling through Congresbury and the surrounding area – his name and deeds are virtually forgotten. Instead, it is his victim whose name has been etched into history … or rather into the granite monument that commemorates his bravery and determination that dark night in late 1830. Taunton played a very small part in their joint story, but one that sealed the highwayman's fate … and there has to be a highwayman.

Some crimes gain a lot of publicity locally but fail to come to the nation's attention, whilst others grab the headlines and pass into history, such as the Yorkshire Ripper case or the 19th century horrors attributed to the anonymous figure recorded as Jack the Ripper. Just occasionally, two names get linked together for the atrocities they have committed, like the Krays, Fred & Rose West, and Ian Brady & Myra Hindley. In the mid-nineteenth century, a married couple became the focus of the nation's attention when they were found guilty of what is now called the Bermondsey Horror, or in its day the Bermondsey Murder.

Frederick and Maria Manning were convicted of the murder of her lover, Patrick O'Connor, for which they paid with their lives. They were hanged together on the roof of Horsemonger Lane Gaol in London on 13 November 1849, the first time a married couple had been executed at the same time in England since 1700. No wonder it caused a stir, but first the bare bones of the matter for anyone unfamiliar with the Mannings.

Maria Manning was a Swiss national who came to Britain and managed to secure posts in the households of families with noble connections. She became enamoured of two men – the man who became her husband and the man who became her lover. O'Connor was equally enthralled by Maria but she decided to marry the younger and better-looking Frederick George Manning instead. However, it could equally be that he seemed a better catch, despite O'Connor being employed at London Docks and having sufficient means or income to have a side-line in money-lending. He became wealthy from the latter business, mostly because of the high interest he charged. When he finally discovered that the object of his desire had married his rival, O'Connor was totally distraught, but then a solution to his despair was offered – Maria would continue to see him, and their relationship turned physical.

Patrick O'Connor was invited to dine with the Mannings on 9th August 1849 in their home at Bermondsey.

He never went home.

He was shot at close range in the back of the head and his body buried under the Mannings' kitchen floor of 3 Miniver Place. The couple departed the premises separately after a couple of days, and a search of their home was only considered after their disappearance became suspicious. Made of flagstones, it was a week later when it was noticed that the kitchen floor had a damp corner stone and on further examination, the earth around it was found to be quite soft. Excavations were made, and O'Connor's body unearthed. The Mannings were sought to explain why their lodgings had become the final resting place of their dinner guest.

On the day the body was discovered, Maria visited O'Connor's lodging just off the Mile End Road in London, and stole his money and railway shares. With more there than she had anticipated, she returned the next day to clear out everything of value. Who knows where she spent the night if their crime was already known to the police, but the couple seem to have been prepared to double-cross each other. With her ill-gotten gains, Maria went north and was tracked down to Edinburgh. She was arrested when she tried to exchange some of the stolen shares, and had others in her possession. Her husband had gone south, taking very little in regard to the spoils of the murder, and he was caught on the island of Jersey.

They were tried at the Old Bailey on 25th and 26th of October, found guilty and sentenced to death. William Calcraft the executioner performed the deed a few weeks later. In the crowd was one Charles Dickens, who later based his character of Mademoiselle Hortense, Lady Dedlock's maid in his novel *Bleak House*, on the life of Maria Manning, thus giving her more immortality than the murder ever could.

So where does Taunton fit into all of this?

Naturally, regional newspapers were full of the case when it happened, regardless of the fact that the action took place in London. These reports would be written with first-hand knowledge of the events rather than writing much later from records that might have been completed at the time. It is not the events of the murder itself that are of concern, but the life of the couple before they settled in Miniver Place.

Frederick George Manning was baptised on the 12th of April 1821 at Taunton St Mary Magdalen. His father was Joseph Manning of

Magdalen Lane, a sergeant in the 1st Somerset Militia, and his
mother's name was Blanch. Joseph, a soldier, married Blanch Ellis in
Cornwall in 1799. With children baptised in Bridgwater, Portsea and
Sussex, he finally settled in Taunton and became a publican.
In 1828, Joseph was the tenant of the Waterloo Inn in High Street
when the inn and other related buildings was placed for sale at auction
(as was the Shakespeare Inn in East Reach at the same event), and the
following year, he was in court charging a couple of teenagers with
theft from the inn. He later ran the Bear Inn in Taunton, as well as
being lessee of market tolls, and of several turnpikes in Taunton and
its surrounds for many years. Not only would Joseph have been much
respected, he would have been able to squirrel away money for a rainy
day, though maybe not as much as people expected - folk such as his
son Frederick.
At the time of Joseph's death, Frederick was employed by the Great
Western Railway as a guard, and his fortunes began to change when
the Colonel of the regiment, Lord Poulet, placed him as a member of
the regimental staff, thus entitling him to an income of ten shillings
and six pence a week. This is supposed to have taken place about
1844/45.

Joseph's burial is recorded in the registers of St Mary Magdalen
church on 24 Sep 1845 at the age of 68 years. He was then resident in
North Street, Taunton, and that is where he was living when the 1841
census was taken. Working as a confectioner, his wife was not listed
with him on census night, but a Charles Manning and a Jane Manning
shared the property, the former matching a son of Joseph and Blanch
(baptised in 1806 in Sussex) and in the same trade as his father.
Charles died two years before his father, and they were both buried in
Taunton. The latter might be Charles' wife or Joseph's daughter.

Blanch Manning was living beyond the Tone Bridge in North Town
with her three youngest children, James, Harriet and Frederick, when
the said census was recorded. She was shown as a toll collector but
this had been crossed through, so perhaps she was estranged from her
husband or, more likely, on census night she just happened to be
staying with others. Her burial in 1848 shows her home address at that
time as North Street.
With his father's reputation to back him, and allegedly with money
from his father's will, Frederick, with money he had managed to save

himself, invested £200 on a mortgage of a small estate not far from Taunton, the deeds of which he deposited with Stuckey's Banking Company. This allowed him to draw £210 from their funds as he was considered to be a well-conducted, responsible young man. He even had recommendations from various contractors in the town who had employed him before he went to work for GWR, some of whom continued to have interests in his welfare and possibly through their backing, he entered into the premises of the White Hart Inn. He had already married Maria by this time. She had indicated that she would soon be rich, and it was possible that he was promising her expected money for the business venture.

Stuckey's Banking Company was formed when three Stuckey ventures – Stuckey, Lean, Hart & Maningford of Bristol; S & G Stuckey of Langport & Stuckey & Woodlands of Bridgwater – amalgamated with the private bank of Ricketts, Thorne & Courtney of Bristol in 1826, to become the second joint stock bank to be formed in the country. All four organisations continued to operate under their own identities for the next two years. Initially based in Langport, and led by Vincent Stuckey, they became a major concern in the West Country as they expanded. Initially they acquired private banks, from Crewkerne, Frome & Trowbridge, Yeovil & Wincanton, Glastonbury & Shepton Mallet, Taunton and Tiverton; the first in 1829, and the last in 1883, before branch and agency openings. In 1908, their head office moved into Taunton, but the following year the name of Stuckey's disappeared after amalgamating with Parr's Bank (and later to become absorbed into Nat West).

A few days after taking control of the White Hart, the town was filled to capacity for the Somerset Spring Assizes, and Frederick Manning's establishment was full to bursting. During that week, he took just under £600 for his business or, to compare it with modern money values, about the equivalent of earning half a million in 2020. This may sound as if he was on the road to riches but he had many debts and promissory notes to consider, items he had found necessary to commit to in order to be the landlord – except some of those funds were nothing but empty myths. Maria's alleged money from her family on the Continent never materialised, and Frederick's was soon expended, probably because it was far less than originally calculated. Notes were starting to be called in, and customers were turning away, preferring other more amiable hostelries in the town. Maria was not a suitable landlady, and the arguments between husband and wife became an embarrassment for their clientele. There were suspicions that Frederick was in some way involved with convicted mail robber, Henry Poole – another reason customers stayed away perhaps. Poole had been dismissed from his employment as a guard on the Great

Western Railway for misconduct, probably on the suspicion that he had been involved in another robbery. He must have worked alongside Frederick Manning at some point, which would explain Poole's fraternisation of Manning's inn. Manning's reason for leaving his post with the railway company is sometimes said to be the result of his own misconduct but is not expanded upon by those choosing to record this reason.

Shady characters were much closer to home. One night, about ten in the evening, Maria packed and left the White Hart, saying she needed to go to the Continent on financial matters to do with her own family. Next morning, her husband made a show of finding his bedroom had been ransacked, with money and other valuables disappearing with her. Did she take them and do a runner? Perhaps this was part of a plan they hatched together to remove anything of value from the premises before goods and cash were seized against the bills and debts owed by Manning, or maybe Maria decided it was time for her to get out with something worthwhile. Her husband was told by those closest to him, and by a solicitor, to call a constable and get his wife apprehended at Southampton before she left the country, but he failed to follow this advice, leaving himself open to the suspicion of being complicit in her disappearance with the things of value. Her departure was hardly unexpected after the way the couple had been acting but his response to her desertion was not typical of a husband wronged by his wife's thievery. Maria was also inately jealous of anything her husband did, and she sought to control him, to the point of denying him access to his elderly mother who lived just yards away, relenting only when the old woman was dying.

The White Hart already had a reputation but of a different kind to that during Manning's tenantry. Standing on the corner of Fore Street and High Street (later to become the site for the Devon & Somerset Stores), it was already a very old house by the time of the Mannings' tenancy there. It was reputed to be the mansion where Colonel Kirk committed his atrocious act. This was after Monmouth's Rebellion, and Kirk had imposed martial law in the area. Described as cruel and impious, the Colonel had people put to death on the slightest of charges, even if they were innocent. Ruling more by fear than the law, one young man was sentenced to death, and his young and beautiful sister begged Kirk to spare his life for her. Kirk agreed to do so if she would yield herself to him. She agreed and spent the night in the Colonel's bed. Next morning, he flung open the shutters and proudly showed her her brother's body swinging from the gibbet in Market Place before laughing in her face. Anger, shame and despair caused the poor girl to take her own life a short time after … or so the legend goes.

Under the terms of his late father's will, Frederick inherited a little more on the death of his mother in 1848. It was not enough to stem the tide of debt he found himself in. The situation between him and Maria grew worse, with Maria locking up his hats and his shoes during her fits of jealousy. Whatever drove the two of them apart, after her departure on the night mail train, it wasn't long before Frederick abandoned the White Hart, either with the help or advice of one of his surviving brothers or by using that brother as a go-between. The brother might even have been used by Frederick as a fall guy, as it was said that the two had fallen out some time before, and the brother was only visiting Taunton but got embroiled in Frederick's financial whirlpool. Eventually, with very little in the way of cash or possessions , Manning left Taunton and went to London where he lodged with another of his brothers.

After new tenants had taken on the White Hart Inn, Maria returned from her trip. She was amazed to find she was not allowed entry to the place, and probably even more surprised to find her husband was long gone. She then followed him to London and must have known of his brother's existence there, as she turned up on their doorstep. Nothing tells of how she was received or what words passed between them but Frederick and Maria lived at a couple of different addresses as man and wife, getting involved with the wealthy Patrick O'Connor, and eventually conniving to murder him. They might have got a more lenient sentence had it not been for the way they tried to cover up their crime.

After shooting O'Connor at close quarters, though who pulled the trigger was never quite clear as each blamed the other, they disposed of the body. Maria had purchased a spade about three weeks prior to the fateful night and the grave was complete well before O'Connor was dead. When O'Connor commented on the obvious hole in her kitchen, Maria told him that the landlord was undertaking work on the drains. By the time Manning said he came downstairs after hearing the shot, O'Connor was already in the pre-dug grave but moaning slightly. He was apparently still alive despite a bullet to his brain.

Frederick took a chisel and battered Patrick's skull until the man was well and truly dead. Maria went through O'Connor's pockets, took a set of keys and announced just twenty minutes after the murder that she could not stay there any longer. She went to O'Connor's lodgings, took shares and came back but noticed she had not got them all. She retrieved the remainder the following day and travelled northwards. Manning stated that he was sent by Maria to change the shares for cash and when he returned, he found the door at Miniver Place locked against him. On enquiring of her whereabouts, he was told Maria had left during his absence, complete with boxes and trunks. So much for their plan to go to America togther! He then makes his way to Jersey., leaving the chisel at Dover Station for collection by a Mrs Smith, who never came to retrieve it because she never actually existed. He told on his arrest of how Maria had picked up a pair of scissors and cut the clothes from O'Connor's body. She then lit a fire and burned them along with their victim's slippers, which exercise lasted into the following day. She produced some lengths of cord and they tied the victim's legs into a position where they were touching his backside before covering the body with lime until it was extremely wet. They then placed it into the grave, and spent a lot time treading down the earth to level the burial place. At midnight they ceased their labours but resumed the next morning before pouring a pint of vitriol over the grave and replacing the flagstones. Maria then planned to continue living there for a year and suggested that he should take a post that had recently been offered to him. The money from selling O'Connor's shares could sustain them, and their continued occupation of the property would allay any suspicions. He did as she bid him but after his first time away with his new job, he came back to find the house locked and his wife and their possessions disappeared into thin air. He then did the same, and their sudden absence led to their home being searched. It was probably thought that the two of them had died together, or some similar gruesome ending. Despite Maria's departure being commented on as part of Manning's explanation of events, nobody thought they would find a body under the kitchen floor, showing a bullet wound and other head injuries and covered with lime – in an attempt to make the corpse decompose more rapidly – except it actually helped to preserve the remains instead.

Frederick George Manning certainly entertained a grudge against Patrick O'Connor, the other man in Maria's life, but his wife seemed to harbour a deep dislike for her lover for not supporting a business venture she had proposed to him. She appears, according to Frederick's confession, to have planned her revenge for several weeks, and was utterly ruthless in eliminating the man she had allowed to be her paramour from the face of the earth.

Maria wore a black satin dress with a long white collar when she was led out to her execution. She had also requested a black veil to cover her head, and to be blindfolded as she was led to the scaffold. This was agreed. In fact, a myth was born that, after her execution, the wearing of black satin went out of fashion for many years … except various fashion catalogues continued to offer the colour, material and style as before.

Her husband, with whom she appears to have spent some time whilst incarcerated in Horsemonger Lane Gaol and the couple seem to have become reconciled as they awaited their fate, was smartly-dressed and walked ahead of her, each of them with a warder on either side, their arms pinioned in regulation fashion for those about to face execution. Frederick's end came quite quickly but Maria lingered for longer. This was not the swift despatch that was perfected by Lincolnshire cobbler, William Marwood. When the Mannings were hanged, the noose was placed around the neck with the knot against the windpipe. Later, under Marwood's instructions after his experimentation outside his workshop with sacks of corn, the knot was placed to the back of the head, against the bottom of the skull. Its position together with the sudden drop, another feature that Marwood had perfected by calculating their height and weight and using an appropriate length of rope, guaranteed a quick despatch by snapping the neck. For Frederick and Maria, and all the others executed in this manner before the method changed (about 1870), they actually died of strangulation as the noose tightened against the throat because of their own body weight. Their executioner, the hangman William Calcraft, disappeared as soon as the two were turned off rather than after they breathed their last . At ten o'clock, their bodies were removed for burial within the grounds of their prison, and the gallows were immediately deconstructed and removed, leaving no trace of what had taken place that fateful morning of 13th November 1849.

Frederick Manning was described as being "handsome" or "good-looking" while, to modern eyes, Maria would be regarded as being overweight. By Victorian standards, she was attractive, chubby and cute, and there are images of the couple from the time of their trial.

Did Maria think about her origins in Lausanne, Switzerland, during her final hours, or perhaps she reflected on her employment with the respectable minor nobility of the 1840s? Maybe Frederick thought about Taunton, his deceased parents, the White Hart Inn, and his family as he passed from this life into eternity …

Henry Poole along with Edward Nightingale were both found guilty of mail train robbery in 1849. Dressed identically, they travelled together in a carriage between Bristol and Exeter and during the journey, they climbed out and made their way to the mail van where they picked up money and jewellery. They then made their way back to their seats but were apprehended at Bridgwater and tried for the offence. They were both sentenced to be transported for 15 years, and being transported meant no way back to England. Anyone returning could be liable to be hanged for doing so. Poole was sent to Bermuda in 1850, and Nightingale to Australia in 1854, some five years into his sentence.

Nightingale's father, George, had been accused of the Dover Mail coach robbery in 1826 but was acquitted. In 1828, he was charged with the assault and robbery of one Richard Crouch at Warwick during a boxing bout that attracted men from all parts of the country. George then accused Crouch, along with two others, of conspiracy in concocting the charge against him. This charge was upheld but the three men were found not guilty. George had been acquitted of the 1826 robbery because he was able to show he was in Tiverton in Devon at the time of the hold-up. Crime and public houses seem to run together as George Nightingale took over the Gun Inn near Holloway, London in 1825, and ran it for the next two years.

Sometimes little snippets of information pop up when you least expect them, and sound interesting. While pursuing the Manning family in Taunton for the previous chapter, a newspaper article came to light in which Joseph Manning, father to Frederick Manning of the Bermondsey Horror notoriety, was the victim of theft by a couple of what we now refer to as teenagers.

The *Taunton Courier & Western Advertiser* printed among, a number of cases at the Somerset Lent Assizes in its edition dated 1 April 1829, the matter of Isaac Hale.

Originally, he was to have been tried for burglary at the previous session of the assizes but for some reason - described as an illness - his case was not heard until these sessions. He was the first prisoner at the bar. and as the details of the charges against him were being brought to the court's attention by Mr Manning (though another account said the charges against Hale were being read out by the Clerk of Arraignments), the young man was suddenly seized by a fit which threw his body into "such violent contortions that it took five or six individuals to restrain him with some difficulty." Perhaps the strain of being in court brought on a fit of epilepsy or Hale was already a sufferer of that particular affliction.

Poor Hale was removed from the dock, probably with little thought for his physical wellbeing, and more by force to get him back to the holding cells as quickly as possible. The Judge consulted with learned counsel about what was the best way to proceed, and discussed Hale's illness with the jailer before making the decision that the lad was to be remanded yet again. Hale was eventually found guilty of the charge on March 28th, and was sentenced to seven years' transportation for burglary and stealing wearing apparel.

He was sent to the hulk "Captivity" to await a fleet to take him and all other undesirables who had been found guilty of a crime to serve their sentences in Australia.

Hulks were used as holding prisons for those to be transported. They were usually old sailing ships that were no longer serviceable for the Royal Navy but were still afloat – just. They were moored at different places along the south coast and in the English Channel. Hale would have been sent to the second ship to bear the name "Captivity" which was moored near the naval station at Portsmouth.

Originally named "Bellerephon", the ship had been launched in 1786 and became a hulk in 1815, her name being changed in 1824. In 1834, the last convicts left her and two years later, the Admiralty sold her. She was subsequently dismantled for scrap.

When enough prisoners had been accommodated in the hulks, a search would be made for suitable ships to transport them to Australia and Van Diemen's Land (now called Tasmania). For Isaac Hale, a spot was found on board the "York" on its first trip carrying 192 convicts and their guards. Two men by the name of Hale were among the convicts – Isaac, who had been employed as a plaisterer, and Thomas Hale, who was tried at Somerset Assizes and sentenced to be transported for life for theft. He died in 1837, accidentally drowned.

Life was a little brighter for Isaac. He was allowed to marry Ann Brooks on 22 Oct 1832 in Hobart, Tasmania, but thereafter, his fate is unknown. His wife was a fellow convict who made the same journey as Isaac aboard the "Providence" on its second trip with convicts. Brooks had been tried in 1825 and sentenced to transportation for life. She had been a prostitute in London and stole a watch from her client, 19 year old baker George Wetton, when she took him back to her rooms for business purposes.

Once in the penal colony in Tasmania, Brooks continued to get into trouble. She would absent herself from her master without permission, and then took to absconding, which, despite the punishment inflicted when she was found, did not stop, even when Hale married her. By 1837, husband and wife were being punished for being drunk, so who knows what happened to them after that.

Her sister, Jane Brooks, was also transported for life in the same year as Ann, and also for life.

At the same sessions in 1829, with Isaac Hale safely in the cells awaiting medical help of some kind, Joseph Manning continued with the case against another 19 year old – Mary Ann Hawker. She was suspected of breaking into Joseph's house and stealing a cloth cloak, a box and other articles – almost the same offence as Isaac Hale … were they partners in crime?

It was the 17th of March 1829 when Manning came downstairs at his hostelry of the Waterloo Inn in Taunton and found somebody had gained entry through a window in the bar area. He noticed things had gone missing – a loaf of bread, some butter, cheese, his daughter's cloak and other items. He made his way to Upottery but the report gave no reason why - unless the fact that Hawker had been employed by Manning as his servant is relevant. There he found Hawker at the local inn and she was wearing the cloak he knew belonged to his daughter. He demanded she take it off. Hawker complied, and then Manning noticed a bundle by her side. On opening it to view its contents, he recognised the items as those taken from his house. He also asked her where the bolts were that fastened the shutters on the bar. He had noticed they were missing, and she told him they had been hidden in one of the outhouses (and where they were later located and returned to their correct function on the shutters).

Hawker was found guilty and sentenced to death.

It might seem very harsh to modern standards to sentence a girl to death for taking some clothes and food but she was living in a time where there was great poverty at one end of the social scale, especially in towns and cities, and great wealth at the top of the social hierarchy. Mary Jane must have been desperate to risk her job as Manning's servant for some bread and cheese, and the fact that the bolts were hidden in an outhouse suggest she removed them as she made her escape from the inn at night, or else she had an accomplice. One of them removed the bolts and secreted them, maybe waiting until she signalled the coast was clear to come and rob the place. However, no mention is made of Manning seeing her with anybody else, and all the items stolen were found in her bundle. This does lend itself to the possibility that Mary Jane was the sole perpetrator of the burglary, and Hale had performed a similar act at Manning's hostelry around the same time.

Whilst the death sentence had been pronounced upon Hawker, this was later commuted to fourteen years' transportation, possibly because of her age, or she showed sufficient contrition for her crime. As a young healthy female, she would have been seen as a nuisance if she remained in England. In prison, she would have to be clothed and fed at the Government's expense, or that of a local authority, and if she fell sick, there would be medical bills to be paid. In Australia, there was a need for females who could help with everyday chores like cooking, cleaning and laundry. Male convicts weren't as skillful with a needle and thread as the women, and both sexes were needed if England was to establish a successful economic and self-sustaining colony on the far side of the world. Transportation emptied the country of miscreants and the sort of low life that walked the streets, corrupting others, whereas putting them onto a ship and sending them as far away as possible meant safer thoroughfares, and it was very much a case of "out of sight, out of mind". Take into consideration that it was men – there were no women administering the law in the 19th century – who tried the criminal cases. They frequently belonged to a better social class, and were generally wealthier, than the poor souls brought into court for committing crimes that were often committed just to survive.

Some of those convicted and sent to the hulks served the whole of their sentences on such vessels, while others never saw Australia, dying on the four month voyage and their body buried at sea. Mary Jane Hawker never managed to leave these shores. She was held in Wilton Gaol until she was sentenced, and then put into Ilchester Gaol where some personal details were recorded. She was 19, single and worked as a servant (to Joseph Manning) living in Taunton. She was five feet and a quarter inch in height, stout with a round face and fresh complexion, She had brown hair and blue eyes with a wart on her left eyelid. Her place of birth was recorded as Fen Ottery.

In July 2nd 1829, she was removed from Ilchester to Millbank Prison in London. It operated to contain convicted prisoners between 1816 and 1890, especially those to be transported. Its position on marshy ground close to the River Thames caused problems with its construction and its design was far from practical. Even after "improvements" were made, it was still an unhealthy environment in which to remain for several years. Millbank also operated the "Separate System" which is best explained as a sort of solitary confinement in the presence of other convicts. Prisoners were not permitted to socialise with each other and occupied cells on their own. Exercise involved walking in the yard for an hour a day, with men having to wear a mask that covered their face and the females had a heavy black veil to disguise their features. No talking was ever allowed between each other, or to prison staff in the presence of other convicts. Even in the prison chapel, they were placed into upright boxes that prevented them from seeing their neighbours to the left or right, and inclined only to see the top of the head of the one in front (but only if you leaned right over, and that was an offence under gaol rules).

Mary Jane Hawker was due to be released on 14 May 1836 but a letter was written about three of the prisoners on 23 August 1832. There was concern for their care, and Hawker was described as "rarely left the Infirmary since her arrival and her constitution is very much shattered".

It has not been possible to determine if she was freed either then or in 1836, or exactly what her eventual fate.

IN THE NEWS

Matters heard in Taunton Police Court:

John Yea, labourer, was charged with stealing an iron crowbar, property of Mr Fish, foreman to Mr Davis, builder, of Taunton on 13 January and George Charles (father of the two children who were committed for trial some short time ago for house-breaking) was charged with receiving it, knowing it to be stolen. Both remanded.

Lucy Saunders, hawker [*pedlar*] was summoned for hawking without having her licence endorsed. A small fine was inflicted.

Somerset County Gazette (23 March 1878 edtn)

A case was called on in which the mayor, who presided, was a witness, and the rosecuting solicitor declined to proceed unless his worship withdrew from the bench. The mayor refused and the solicitor then stated his worship had intimidated the prosecutor with a view to getting him to settle the case. This his worship indignantly denied, and after an unpleasant scene the case was adjourned to enable the Home Secretary to be communicated with.

South Wales Echo (3 August 1887 edtn)

In 1887, the Mayor of Taunton was Dr Samuel Farrant, then in his third term in office. He died at his country residence at Pitminster in 1903, age 65 years. Two of his four sons followed in his footsteps – Sydney became Surgeon at Taunton Hospital, a post once held by his father, and Rupert became a general surgeon with a practice in London, with an interest in afflictions of the thyroid. Rupert served in the Royal Army Medical Corps during WW1 as a captain, and was injured in a shell explosion as well as suffering trench fever and nephritis during his service, for which he was awarded the Military Cross for gallantry. Returning to his practice after the war, it became evident his wartime experiences had a much greater affect upon him than anticipated and probably led to his suicide at Kilburn Park station in January 1921, aged 37 years.

Henry Matthews, MP for Birmingham East, was Home Secretary in 1887 under Lord Salisbury's second government. Leader of the opposition at the time was William Ewart Gladstone.

Lightning Source UK Ltd.
Milton Keynes UK
UKHW040620200522
403285UK00001B/96

9 781803 024974